SARA SULERI was educated in Pakistan, England and the United States. She is currently Associate Professor of English at Yale University. For "Excellent Things in Women", the first chapter of this book, she was awarded the 1987 Pushcart Prize. She has also published *The Rhetoric of English India*.

## Extracts from the reviews of *Meatless Days*

"*Meatless Days* is so much more than mere memoir. It is a profound meditation on women's lives, and on men's, on love and food and introspection, on sexuality and imagination . . . both rare and refreshing."

JOHN HOLLANDER

"This remarkable memoir . . . is like the unpronounceable entrée we might order at an exotic restaurant. When it arrives, the sauce seems strange, an irritant to the tongue; but cooked in it, to perfection, are little chunks of meat with an irresistible flavour of their own. We know that, in days to come, we will be at that exotic restaurant again, asking for what is, now, an unforgettable name."

FIRDAUS KANGA, *Sunday Times*

"*Meatless Days* is chiefly notable for its sense of loss, but at the same time it is achingly funny."

D. J. TAYLOR, *Independent*

"The glory of this volume is its use of language. Suleri has colonized the English language on her own terms. Her tone throughout is indulgently affectionate, but with mordant laughter and ironic bite."

FRANCINE CUNNINGHAM, *Irish Times*

# MEATLESS DAYS

Sara Suleri

Flamingo

*An Imprint of HarperCollins Publishers*

Flamingo
An Imprint of HarperCollins*Publishers*
77–85 Fulham Palace Road,
Hammersmith, London W6 8JB

Published by Flamingo 1991
3 5 7 9 8 6 4 2

First published in the United States by
The University of Chicago Press, 1989

First published in the UK by
William Collins Sons & Co. Ltd, 1990

Copyright © by the University of Chicago 1989

Sara Suleri asserts the moral right to
be identified as the author of this work

ISBN 0 00 654389 8

Printed in Great Britain by
Clays Ltd, St Ives plc

# CONTENTS

# EXCELLENT THINGS
# IN WOMEN

Leaving Pakistan was, of course, tantamount to giving up the company of women. I can tell this only to someone like Anita, in all the faith that she will understand, as we go perambulating through the grimness of New Haven and feed on the pleasures of our conversational way. Dale, who lives in Boston, would also understand. She will one day write a book about the stern and secretive life of breast-feeding and is partial to fantasies that culminate in an abundance of resolution. And Fawzi, with a grimace of recognition, knows because she knows the impulse to forget.

To a stranger or an acquaintance, however, some vestigial remoteness obliges me to explain that my reference is to a place where the concept of woman was not really part of an available vocabulary: we were too busy for that, just living, and conducting precise negotiations with what it meant to be a sister or a child or a wife or a mother or a servant. By this point admittedly I am damned by my own discourse, and doubly damned when I add yes, once in a while, we naturally thought of ourselves as women, but only in some perfunctory biological way that we happened on perchance. Or else it was a hugely practical joke, we thought, hidden somewhere among our clothes. But formulating that definition is about

1

as impossible as attempting to locate the luminous qualities of an Islamic landscape, which can on occasion generate such aesthetically pleasing moments of life. My audience is lost, and angry to be lost, and both of us must find some token of exchange for this failed conversation. I try to lay the subject down and change its clothes, but before I know it, it has sprinted off evilly in the direction of ocular evidence. It goads me into saying, with the defiance of a plea, "You did not deal with Dadi."

Dadi, my father's mother, was born in Meerut toward the end of the last century. She was married at sixteen and widowed in her thirties, and by her latter decades could never exactly recall how many children she had borne. When India was partitioned, in August of 1947, she moved her thin pure Urdu into the Punjab of Pakistan and waited for the return of her eldest son, my father. He had gone careening off to a place called Inglestan, or England, fired by one of the several enthusiasms made available by the proliferating talk of independence. Dadi was peeved. She had long since dispensed with any loyalties larger than the pitiless give-and-take of people who are forced to live together in the same place, and she resented independence for the distances it made. She was not among those who, on the fourteenth of August, unfurled flags and festivities against the backdrop of people running and cities burning. About that era she would only say, looking up sour and cryptic over the edge of her Quran, "And I was also burned." She was, but that came years later.

By the time I knew her, Dadi with her flair for drama had allowed life to sit so heavily upon her back that her spine wilted and froze into a perfect curve, and so it was in the posture of a shrimp that she went scuttling through the day. She either scuttled or did not: it all depended on the nature of her fight with the Devil. There were days when she so hated him that all she could do was stretch herself out straight and tiny on her bed, uttering most awful imprecation. Sometimes, to my mother's great distress, Dadi could berate Satan

2

in full eloquence only after she had clambered on top of the dining-room table and lain there like a little molding center-piece. Satan was to blame: he had after all made her older son linger long enough in Inglestan to give up his rightful wife, a cousin, and take up instead with a white-legged woman. Satan had stolen away her only daughter Ayesha when Ayesha lay in childbirth. And he'd sent her youngest son to Swaziland, or Switzerland; her thin hand waved away such sophistries of name.

God she loved, and she understood him better than any-one. Her favorite days were those when she could circum-navigate both the gardener and my father, all in the solemn service of her God. With a pilfered knife, she'd wheedle her way to the nearest sapling in the garden, some sprightly poplar or a newly planted eucalyptus. She'd squat, she'd hack it down, and then she'd peel its bark away until she had a walking stick, all white and virgin and her own. It drove my father into tears of rage. He must have bought her a dozen walking sticks, one for each of our trips to the mountains, but it was like assembling a row of briar pipes for one who will not smoke: Dadi had different aims. Armed with implements of her own creation, she would creep down the driveway unper-ceived to stop cars and people on the street and give them all the gossip that she had on God.

Food, too, could move her to intensities. Her eyesight always took a sharp turn for the worse over meals—she could point hazily at a perfectly ordinary potato and murmur with Adamic reverence "What is it, what is it called?" With some shortness of manner one of us would describe and catalog the items on the table. "*Alu ka bhartha*," Dadi repeated with wonderment and joy; "Yes, Saira Begum, you can put some here." "Not too much," she'd add pleadingly. For ritual had it that the more she demurred, the more she expected her plate to be piled with an amplitude her own politeness would never allow. The ritual happened three times a day.

We pondered it but never quite determined whether food or God constituted her most profound delight. Ob-

3

vious problems, however, occurred whenever the two converged. One such occasion was the Muslim festival called Eid—not the one that ends the month of fasting, but the second Eid, which celebrates the seductions of the Abraham story in a remarkably literal way. In Pakistan, at least, people buy sheep or goats beforehand and fatten them up for weeks with delectables. Then, on the appointed day, the animals are chopped, in place of sons, and neighbors graciously exchange silver trays heaped with raw and quivering meat. Following Eid prayers the men come home, and the animal is killed, and shortly thereafter rush out of the kitchen steaming plates of grilled lung and liver, of a freshness quite superlative.

It was a freshness to which my Welsh mother did not immediately take. She observed the custom but discerned in it a conundrum that allowed no ready solution. Liberal to an extravagant degree on thoughts abstract, she found herself to be remarkably squeamish about particular things. Chopping up animals for God was one. She could not locate the metaphor and was uneasy when obeisance played such a truant to the metaphoric realm. My father the writer quite agreed: he was so civilized in those days.

Dadi didn't agree. She pined for choppable things. Once she made the mistake of buying a baby goat and bringing him home months in advance of Eid. She wanted to guarantee the texture of his festive flesh by a daily feeding of tender peas and clarified butter. Ifat, Shahid, and I greeted a goat into the family with boisterous rapture, and soon after he ravished us completely when we found him at the washingline nonchalantly eating Shahid's pajamas. Of course there was no argument: the little goat was our delight, and even Dadi knew there was no killing him. He became my brother's and my sister's and my first pet, and he grew huge, a big and grinning thing.

Years after, Dadi had her will. We were old enough, she must have thought, to set the house sprawling, abstracted, into a multitude of secrets. This was true, but still we all noticed one another's secretive ways. When, the day before Eid, our Dadi disappeared, my brothers and sisters and I just shook our heads. We hid the fact from my father, who at this time of life had begun to equate petulance with extreme vociferation. So we went about our jobs and tried to be Islamic for a day. We waited to sight moons on the wrong occasion, and watched the food come into lavishment. Dried dates change shape when they are soaked in milk, and carrots rich and strange turn magically sweet when deftly covered with green nutty shavings and smatterings of silver. Dusk was sweet as we sat out, the day's work done, in an evening garden. Lahore spread like peace around us. My father spoke, and when Papa talked, it was of Pakistan. But we were glad, then, at being audience to that familiar conversation, till his voice looked up, and failed. There was Dadi making her return, and she was prodigal. Like a question mark interested only in its own conclusions, her body crawled through the gates. Our guests were spellbound, then they looked away. Dadi, moving in her eerie crab formations, ignored the hangman's rope she firmly held as behind her in the gloaming minced, hugely affable, a goat.

That goat was still smiling the following day when Dadi's victory brought the butcher, who came and went just as he should on Eid. The goat was killed and cooked: a scrawny beast that required much cooking and never melted into succulence, he winked and glistened on our plates as we sat eating him on Eid. Dadi ate, that is: Papa had taken his mortification to some distant corner of the house; Ifat refused to chew on hemp; Tillat and Irfan gulped their baby sobs over such a slaughter. "Honestly," said Mamma, "honestly." For Dadi had successfully cut through tissues of festivity just as the butcher slit the goat, but there was something else that she was eating with that meat. I saw it in her concentration; I know that she was making God talk to her as to Abraham and was showing him what she could do—for him—to sons. God didn't dare, and she ate on alone.

Of those middle years it is hard to say whether Dadi was

literally left alone or whether her bodily presence always emanated a quality of being apart and absorbed. In the winter I see her alone, painstakingly dragging her straw mat out to the courtyard at the back of the house and following the rich course of the afternoon sun. With her would go her Quran, a metal basin in which she could wash her hands, and her ridiculously heavy spouted waterpot, that was made of brass. None of us, according to Dadi, were quite pure enough to transport these particular items, but the rest of her paraphernalia we were allowed to carry out. These were baskets of her writing and sewing materials and her bottle of pungent and Dadi-like bitter oils, with which she'd coat the papery skin that held her brittle bones. And in the summer, when the night created an illusion of possible coolness and everyone held their breath while waiting for a thin and intermittent breeze, Dadi would be on the roof, alone. Her summer bed was a wooden frame latticed with a sweet-smelling rope, much aerated at its foot. She'd lie there all night until the wild monsoons would wake the lightest and the soundest sleeper into a rapturous welcome of rain.

In Pakistan, of course, there is no spring but only a rapid elision from winter into summer, which is analogous to the absence of a recognizable loneliness from the behavior of that climate. In a similar fashion it was hard to distinguish between Dadi with people and Dadi alone: she was merely impossibly unable to remain unnoticed. In the winter, when she was not writing or reading, she would sew for her delight tiny and magical reticules out of old silks and fragments she had saved, palm-sized cloth bags that would unravel into the precision of secret and more secret pockets. But none such pockets did she ever need to hide, since something of Dadi always remained intact, however much we sought to open her. Her discourse, for example, was impervious to penetration, so that when one or two of us remonstrated with her in a single hour, she never bothered to distinguish her replies. Instead she would pronounce generically and prophetically, "The world takes on a single face." "Must you, Dadi . . . ,"

I'd begin, to be halted then by her great complaint: "The world takes on a single face."

It did. And often it was a countenance of some delight, for Dadi also loved the accidental jostle with things belligerent. As she went perambulating through the house, suddenly she'd hear Shahid, her first grandson, telling me or one of my sisters we were vile, we were disgusting women. And Dadi, who never addressed any one of us girls without first conferring the title of lady—so we were "Teellat Begum," "Nuzhat Begum," "Iffatt Begum," "Saira Begum"— would halt in reprimand and tell her grandson never to call her granddaughters women. "What else shall I call them, men?" Shahid yelled. "Men!" said Dadi, "Men! There is more goodness in a woman's little finger than in the benighted mind of man." "Hear, hear, Dadi! *Hanh, hanh,* Dadi!" my sisters cried. "For men," said Dadi, shaking the name off her fingertips like some unwanted water, "live as though they were unsuckled things." "And heaven," she grimly added, "is the thing Muhammad says (peace be upon him) lies beneath the feet of women!" "But he was a man," Shahid still would rage, if he weren't laughing, as all of us were laughing, while Dadi sat among us as a belle or a May queen

Toward the end of the middle years my father stopped speaking to his mother, and the atmosphere at home appreciably improved. They secretly hit upon a novel histrionics that took the place of their daily battle. They chose the curious way of silent things: twice a day Dadi would leave her room and walk the long length of the corridor to my father's room. There she merely peered round the door, as though to see if he were real. Each time she peered, my father would interrupt whatever adult thing he might be doing in order to enact a silent paroxysm, an elaborate facial pantomime of revulsion and affront. At teatime in particular, when Papa would want the world to congregate in his room, Dadi came to peer her ghostly peer. Shortly thereafter conversation was bound to fracture, for we could not drown the fact that Dadi, invigorated by an outcast's strength, was sitting alone in the dining room, chanting an appeal: "God give me tea, God give me tea."

At about this time Dadi stopped smelling old and smelled instead of something equivalent to death. It would have been easy to notice if she had been dying, but instead she conducted the change as a refinement, a subtle gradation, just as her annoying little stove could shift its hanging odors away from smoke and into ash. During the middle years there had been something more defined about her being, which sat in the world as solely its own context. But Pakistan increasingly complicated the question of context, as though history, like a pestilence, forbid any definition outside relations to its fevered sleep. So it was simple for my father to ignore the letters that Dadi had begun to write to him every other day in her fine wavering script, letters of advice about the house or the children or the servants. Or she transcribed her complaint: "Oh my son, Zia. Do you think your son, Shahid, upon whom God bestow a thousand blessings, should be permitted to lift up his grandmother's chair and carry it into the courtyard when his grandmother is seated in it?" She had cackled in a combination of delight and virgin joy when Shahid had so transported her, but that little crackling sound she omitted from her letter. She ended it, and all her notes, with her single endearment. It was a phrase to halt and arrest when Dadi actually uttered it: her solitary piece of tenderness was an injunction, really, to her world—"Keep on living," she would say.

Between that phrase and the great Dadi conflagration comes the era of the trying times. They began in the winter war of 1971, when East Pakistan became Bangladesh and Indira Gandhi hailed the demise of the two-nation theory. Ifat's husband was off fighting, and we spent the war together with her father-in-law, the brigadier, in the pink house on the hill. It was an ideal location for antiaircraft guns, so there was a bevy of soldiers and weaponry installed upon our roof. During each air raid the brigadier would stride purposefully into the garden and bark commands at them, as though the crux of the war rested upon his stiff upper lip. Then Dacca fell, and General Yahya came on television to resign the presidency and concede defeat. "Drunk, by God!" barked the brigadier as we sat watching, "Drunk!"

The following morning General Yahya's mistress came to mourn with us over breakfast, lumbering in draped with swathes of overscented silk. The brigadier lit an English cigarette—he was frequently known to avow that Pakistani cigarettes gave him a cuff—and bit on his moustache. "Yes," he barked, "these are trying times." "Oh yes, Gul," Yahya's mistress wailed, "these are such trying times." She gulped on her own eloquence, her breakfast bosom quaked, and then resumed authority over that dangling sentence: "It is so trying," she continued, "I find it so trying, it is trying to us all, to live in these trying, trying times." Ifat's eyes met mine in complete accord: mistress transmogrified to muse; Bhutto returned from the UN to put Yahya under house arrest and become the first elected president of Pakistan; Ifat's husband went to India as a prisoner of war for two years; my father lost his newspaper. We had entered the era of the trying times.

Dadi didn't notice the war, just as she didn't really notice the proliferation of her great-grandchildren, for Ifat and Nuzzi conceived at the drop of a hat and kept popping babies out for our delight. Tillat and I felt favored at this vicarious taste of motherhood: we learned to become that enviable personage, a *khala*, mother's sister, and when our married sisters came to visit with their entourage, we reveled in the exercise of *khala*-love. I once asked Dadi how many sisters she had had. She looked up through the oceanic grey of her cataracted eyes and answered, "I forget."

The children helped, because we needed distraction, there being then in Pakistan a musty taste of defeat to all our activities. The children gave us something, but they also took something away—they initiated a slight displacement of my mother. Because her grandchildren would not speak any English, she could not read stories as of old. Urdu always remained a shyness on her tongue, and as the babies came and went she let something of her influence imperceptibly recede, as though she occupied an increasingly private space. Her eldest son was in England by then, so Mamma found herself assuming the classic posture of an Indian woman who sends away her sons and runs the risk of seeing them succumb to the great alternatives represented by the West. It was a position that preoccupied her; and without my really noticing what was happening, she quietly handed over many of her wifely duties to her two remaining daughters—to Tillat and to me. In the summer, once the ferocity of the afternoon sun had died down, it was her pleasure to go out into the garden on her own. There she would stand, absorbed and abstracted, watering the driveway and breathing in the heady smell of water on hot dust. I'd watch her often, from my room upstairs. She looked like a girl.

We were aware of something, of a reconfiguration in the air, but could not exactly tell where it would lead us. Dadi now spoke mainly to herself; even the audience provided by the deity had dropped away. Somehow there wasn't a proper balance between the way things came and the way they went, as Halima the cleaning woman knew full well when she looked at me intently, asking a question that had no question in it: "Do I grieve, or do I celebrate?" Halima had given birth to her latest son the night her older child died in screams of meningitis; once heard, never to be forgotten. She came back to work a week later, and we were talking as we put away the family's winter clothes into vast metal trunks. For in England, they would call it spring.

We felt a quickening urgency of change drown our sense of regular direction, as though something were bound to happen soon but not knowing what it would be was making history nervous. And so we were not really that surprised, then, to find ourselves living through the summer of the trials by fire. It climaxed when Dadi went up in a little ball of flames, but somehow sequentially related were my mother's trip to England to tend her dying mother, and the night I beat up Tillat, and the evening I nearly castrated my little brother, runt of the litter, serious-eyed Irfan.

It was an accident on both our parts. I was in the kitchen, so it must have been a Sunday, when Allah Ditta the cook took the evenings off. He was a mean-spirited man with an incongruously delicate touch when it came to making food. On Sunday at midday he would bluster one of us into the kitchen and show us what he had prepared for the evening meal, leaving strict and belligerent instructions about what would happen if we overheated this or dared brown that. So I was in the kitchen heating up some food when Farni came back from playing hockey, an ominous asthmatic rattle in his throat. He, the youngest, had been my parents' gravest infant: in adolescence he remained a gentle invalid. Of course he pretended otherwise, and was loud and raucous, but it never worked.

Tillat and I immediately turned on him with the bullying litany that actually can be quite soothing, the invariable female reproach to the returning male. He was to do what he hated—stave off his disease by sitting over a bowl of camphor and boiling water and inhaling its acrid fumes. I insisted that he sit on the cook's little stool in the kitchen, holding the bowl of medicated water on his lap, so that I could cook, and Farni could not cheat, and I could time each minute he should sit there thus confined. We seated him and flounced a towel on his reluctant head. The kitchen reeked jointly of cumin and camphor, and he sat skinny and penitent and swathed for half a minute, and then was begging to be done. I slammed down the carving knife and screamed "Irfan!" with such ferocity that he jumped, figuratively and literally, right out of his skin. The bowl of water emptied onto him, and with a gurgling cry Irfan leapt up, tearing at his steaming clothes. He clutched at his groin, and everywhere he touched, the skin slid off, so that between his fingers his penis easily unsheathed, a blanched and fiery grape. "What's happening?" screamed Papa from his room; "What's happening?" echoed Dadi's wail from the opposite end of the house. What was happening was that I was holding Farni's shoulders, trying to stop him from jumping up and down, but I was jumping too, while Tillat just stood there frozen, frowning at his poor ravaged grapes.

This was June, and the white heat of summer. We spent the next few days laying ice on Farni's wounds: half the time I was allowed to stay with him, until the doctors suddenly remembered I was a woman and hurried me out when his body made crazy spastic reactions to its burns. Once things grew calmer and we were alone, Irfan looked away and said, "I hope I didn't shock you, Sara." I was so taken by tenderness for his bony convalescent body that it took me years to realize yes, something female in me had been deeply shocked.

Mamma knew nothing of this, of course. We kept it from her so she could concentrate on what had taken her back to the rocky coastline of Wales, to places she had not really revisited since she was a girl. She sat waiting with her mother, who was blind now and of a fine translucency, and both of them knew that they were waiting for her death. It was a peculiar posture for Mamma to maintain, but her quiet letters spoke mainly of the sharp astringent light that made the sea wind feel so brisk in Wales and so many worlds away from the deadly omnipresent weight of summer in Lahore. There in Wales one afternoon, walking childless among the brambles and the furze, Mamma realized that her childhood was distinctly lost. "It was not that I wanted to feel more familiar," she later told me, "or that I was more used to feeling unfamiliar in Lahore. It's just that familiarity isn't important, really," she murmured absently, "it really doesn't matter at all."

When Mamma was ready to return, she wired us her plans, and my father read the cable, kissed it, then put it in his pocket. I watched him and felt startled, as we all did on the occasions when our parents' lives seemed to drop away before our eyes, leaving them youthfully engrossed in the illusion of knowledge conferred by love. We were so used to conceiving of them as parents moving in and out of hectic days that it always amused us, and touched us secretly, when they made quaint and punctilious returns to the amorous bond that had initiated their unlikely life together.

That summer while my mother was away, Tillat and I experienced a new bond of powerlessness, the white and shaking rage of sexual jealousy in parenthood. I had always behaved toward her as a contentious surrogate parent, but she had been growing beyond that scope and in her girlhood asking me for a formal acknowledgment of equality that I was loath to give. My reluctance was rooted in a helpless fear of what the world might do to her, for I was young and ignorant enough not to see that what I might do was worse. She went out one evening when my father was off on one of his many trips. The house was gaping emptily, and Tillat was very late. Allah Ditta had gone home, and Dadi and Irfan were sleeping; I read, and thought, and walked up and down the garden, and Tillat was very, very late. When she came back she wore that strange sheath of complacency and guilt which pleasure puts on faces very young. It smote an outrage in my heart until despite all resolutions to the contrary I heard myself hiss: "And where were you?" Her returning look was fearful and preening at the same time, and the next thing to be smitten was her face. "Don't, Sara," Tillat said in her superior way, "physical violence is so degrading." "To you, maybe," I answered, and hit her once again.

It set a sorrowful bond between us, for we both felt complicit in the shamefulness that had made me seem righteous whereas I had felt simply jealous, which we tacitly agreed was a more legitimate thing to be. But we had lost something, a certain protective aura, some unspoken myth asserting that love between sisters at least was sexually innocent. Now we had to fold that vain belief away and stand in more naked relation to our affection. Till then we had associated such violence with all that was outside us, as though somehow the more history fractured, the more whole we would be. But we began to lose that sense of the differentiated identities of history and ourselves and became guiltily aware that we had known it all along, our part in the construction of unreality.

By this time, Dadi's burns were slowly learning how to heal. It was she who had given the summer its strange pace by nearly burning herself alive at its inception. On an early April night Dadi awoke, seized by a desperate need for tea. It was three in the morning, the household was asleep, so she was free to do the great forbidden thing of creeping into Allah Ditta's kitchen and taking charge, like a pixie in the night. As all of us had grown bored of predicting, one of her many cotton garments took to fire that truant night. Dadi, however, deserves credit for her resourceful voice, which wavered out for witness to her burning death. By the time Tillat awoke and found her, she was a little flaming ball: "Dadi!" cried Tillat in the reproach of sleep, and beat her quiet with a blanket. In the morning we discovered that Dadi's torso had been almost consumed and little recognizable remained from collarbone to groin. The doctors bade us to some decent mourning.

But Dadi had different plans. She lived through her sojourn at the hospital; she weathered her return. Then, after six weeks at home, she angrily refused to be lugged like a chunk of meat to the doctor's for her daily change of dressings: "Saira Begum will do it," she announced. Thus developed my great intimacy with the fluid properties of human flesh. By the time Mamma left for England, Dadi's left breast was still coagulate and raw. Later, when Irfan got his burns, Dadi was growing pink and livid tightropes, strung from hip to hip in a flaming advertisement of life. And in the days when Tillat and I were wrestling, Dadi's vanished nipples started to congeal and convex their cavities into triumphant little love knots.

I learned about the specialization of beauty through that body. There were times, as with love, when I felt only disappointment, carefully easing off the dressings and finding again a piece of flesh that would not knit, happier in the

14

texture of stubborn glue. But then on more exhilarating days I'd peel like an onion all her bandages away and suddenly discover I was looking down at some literal tenacity and was bemused at all the freshly withered shapes she could create. Each new striation was a victory to itself, and when Dadi's hairless groin solidified again and sent firm signals that her abdomen must do the same, I could have wept with glee.

After her immolation, Dadi's diet underwent some curious changes. At first her consciousness teetered too much for her to pray, but then as she grew stronger it took us a while to notice what was missing: she had forgotten prayer. It left her life as firmly as tobacco can leave the lives of only the most passionate smokers, and I don't know if she ever prayed again. At about this time, however, with the heavy-handed inevitability that characterized his relation to his mother, my father took to prayer. I came home one afternoon and looked for him in all the usual places, but he wasn't to be found. Finally I came across Tillat and asked her where Papa was. "Praying," she said. *"Praying?"* I said. "Praying," she said, and I felt most embarrassed. For us it was rather as though we had come upon the children playing some forbidden titillating game and decided it was wisest to ignore it calmly. In an unspoken way, though, I think we dimly knew we were about to witness Islam's departure from the land of Pakistan. The men would take it to the streets and make it vociferate, but the great romance between religion and the populace, the embrace that engendered Pakistan, was done. So Papa prayed, with the desperate ardor of a lover trying to converse life back into a finished love.

That was a change, when Dadi patched herself together again and forgot to put prayer back into its proper pocket, for God could now leave the home and soon would join the government. Papa prayed and fasted and went on pilgrimage and read the Quran aloud with most peculiar locutions. Occasionally we also caught him in nocturnal altercations that made him sound suspiciously like Dadi: we looked askance, but didn't say a thing. My mother was altogether admirable: she behaved as though she'd always known that she'd wed a swaying, chanting thing and that to register surprise now would be an impoliteness to existence. Her expression reminded me somewhat of the time when Ifat was eight and Mamma was urging her recalcitrance into some goodly task. Ifat postponed, and Mamma, always nifty with appropriate fables, quoted meaningfully: " 'I'll do it myself,' said the little red hen." Ifat looked up with bright affection. "Good little red hen," she murmured. Then a glance crossed my mother's face, a look between a slight smile and a quick rejection of the eloquent response, like a woman looking down and then away.

She looked like that at my father's sudden hungering for God, which was added to the growing number of subjects about which we, my mother and her daughters, silently decided we had no conversation. We knew there was something other than trying times ahead and would far rather hold our breath than speculate about what other surprises the era held up its capacious sleeve. Tillat and I decided to quash our dread of waiting around for change by changing for ourselves, before destiny took the time to come our way. I would move to America, and Tillat to Kuwait and marriage. To both declarations of intention my mother said "I see," and helped us in our preparations: she knew by then her elder son would not return, and was prepared to extend the courtesy of change to her daughters, too. We left, and Islam predictably took to the streets, shaking Bhutto's empire. Mamma and Dadi remained the only women in the house, the one untalking, the other unpraying.

Dadi behaved abysmally at my mother's funeral, they told me, and made them all annoyed. She set up loud and unnecessary lamentations in the dining room, somewhat like an heir apparent, as though this death had reinstated her as mother of the house. While Ifat and Nuzzi and Tillat wandered frozen-eyed, dealing with the roses and the ice, Dadi demanded an irritating amount of attention, stretching out supine and crying out, "Your mother has betrayed your father; she has left him; she has gone." Food from respectful mourners poured in, caldron after caldron, and Dadi relocated a voracious appetite.

Years later, I was somewhat sorry that I had heard this tale, because it made me take affront. When I returned to Pakistan, I was too peeved with Dadi to find out how she was. Instead I listened to Ifat tell me about standing there in the hospital, watching the doctors suddenly pump upon my mother's heart— "I'd seen it on television," she gravely said, "I knew it was the end." Mamma's students from the university had tracked down the rickshaw driver who had knocked her down: they'd pummeled him nearly to death and then camped out in our garden, sobbing wildly, all in hordes.

By this time Bhutto was in prison and awaiting trial, and General Zulu was presiding over the Islamization of Pakistan. But we had no time to notice. My mother was buried at the nerve center of Lahore, an unruly and dusty place, and my father immediately made arrangements to buy the plot of land next to her grave: "We're ready when you are," Shahid sang. Her tombstone bore some pretty Urdu poetry and a completely fictitious place of birth, because some details my father tended to forget. "Honestly," it would have moved his wife to say.

So I was angry with Dadi at that time and didn't stop to see her. I saw my mother's grave and then came back to America, hardly noticing when, six months later, my father called from London and mentioned Dadi was now dead. It happened in the same week that Bhutto finally was hanged, and our imaginations were consumed by that public and historical dying. Pakistan made rapid provisions not to talk about the thing that had been done, and somehow, accidently, Dadi must have been mislaid into that larger decision, because she too ceased being a mentioned thing. My father tried to get back in time for the funeral, but he was so busy talking Bhutto-talk in England that he missed his flight and thus did not return. Luckily, Irfani was at home, and he saw Dadi to her grave.

Bhutto's hanging had the effect of making Pakistan feel unreliable, particularly to itself. Its landscape learned a new secretiveness, unusual for a formerly loquacious people. This may account for the fact that I have never seen my grandmother's grave and neither have my sisters. I think we would have tried, had we been together, despite the free-floating anarchy in the air that—like the heroin trade—made the world suspicious and afraid. There was no longer any need to wait for change, because change was all there was, and we had quite forgotten the flavor of an era that stayed in place long enough to gain a name. One morning I awoke to find that, during the course of the night, my mind had completely ejected the names of all the streets in Pakistan, as though to assure that I could not return, or that if I did, it would be returning to a loss. Overnight the country had grown absentminded, and patches of amnesia hung over the hollows of the land like fog.

I think we would have mourned Dadi in our belated way, but the coming year saw Ifat killed in the consuming rush of change and disbanded the company of women for all time. It was a curious day in March, two years after my mother died, when the weight of that anniversary made us all disconsolate for her quietude. "I'll speak to Ifat, though," I thought to myself in America. But in Pakistan someone had different ideas for that sister of mine and thwarted all my plans. When she went walking out that warm March night, a car came by and trampled her into the ground, and then it vanished strangely. By the time I reached Lahore, a tall and slender mound had usurped the grave-space where my father had hoped to lie, next to the more moderate shape that was his wife. Children take over everything.

So, worn by repetition, we stood by Ifat's grave, and took note of the narcissi, still alive, that she must have placed upon my mother on the day that she was killed. It made us impatient, in a way, as though we had to decide that there was nothing so farcical as grief and that it had to be eliminated from our diets for good. It cut away, of course, our intimacy with Pakistan, where history is synonymous with grief and always most at home in the attitudes of grieving. Our congregation in Lahore was brief, and then we swiftly returned to a more geographic reality. "We are lost, Sara," Shahid said to me on the phone from England. "Yes, Shahid," I firmly said, "We're lost."

Today, I'd be less emphatic. Ifat and Mamma must have honeycombed and crumbled now, in the comfortable way that overtakes bedfellows. And somehow it seems apt and heartening that Dadi, being what she was, never suffered the pomposities that enter the most well-meaning of farewells and seeped instead into the nooks and crannies of our forgetfulness. She fell between two stools of grief, which is appropriate, since she was greatest when her life was at its most unreal. Anyway she was always outside our ken, an anecdotal thing, neither more nor less. So some sweet reassurance of reality accompanies my discourse when I claim that when Dadi died, we all forgot to grieve.

For to be lost is just a minute's respite, after all, like a train that cannot help but stop between the stations of its proper destination in order to stage a pretend version of the end. Dying, we saw, was simply change taken to points of mocking extremity, and wasn't a thing to lose us but to find us out, to catch us where we least wanted to be caught. In Pakistan, Bhutto rapidly became obsolete after a succession of bumper harvests, and none of us can fight the ways that the names Mamma and Ifat have become archaisms, quaintnesses on our lips.

Now I live in New Haven and feel quite happy with my life. I miss, of course, the absence of women and grow increasingly nostalgic for a world where the modulations of age are as recognized and welcomed as the shift from season into season. But that's a hazard that has to come along, since I have made myself inhabitant of a population which democratically insists that everyone from twenty-nine to fifty-six occupies roughly the same space of age. When I teach topics in third world literature, much time is lost in trying to explain that the third world is locatable only as a discourse of convenience. Trying to find it is like pretending that history or home is real and not located precisely where you're sitting, I hear my voice quite idiotically say. And then it happens. A face, puzzled and attentive and belonging to my gender, raises its intelligence to question why, since I am teaching third world writing, I haven't given equal space to women writers on my syllabus. I look up, the horse's mouth, a foolish thing to be. Unequal images battle in my mind for precedence—there's imperial Ifat, there's Mamma in the garden, and Halima the cleaning woman is there too, there's uncanny Dadi with her goat. Against all my own odds I know what I must say. Because, I'll answer slowly, there are no women in the third world.

# MEATLESS DAYS

I had strongly hoped that they would say sweetbreads instead of testicles, but I was wrong. The only reason it had become a question in my mind was Tillat's fault, of course: she had come visiting from Kuwait one summer, arriving in New Haven with her three children, all of them designed to constitute a large surprise. As a surprise it worked wonderfully, leaving me reeling with the shock of generation that attends on infants and all the detail they manage to accrue. But the end of the day would come at last, and when the rhythm of their sleep sat like heavy peace upon a room, then Tillat and I could talk. Our conversations were meals, delectable, but fraught with a sense of prior copyright, because each of us was obliged to talk too much about what the other did not already know. Speaking over and across the separation of our lives, we discovered that there was an internal revenue involved in so much talking, so much listening. One evening my sister suddenly remembered to give me a piece of information that she had been storing up, like a squirrel, through the long desert months of the previous year. Tillat at twenty-seven had arrived at womanhood with comparatively little fuss—or so her aspect says—and her astonishing recall of my mother's face has always seemed to owe

21

more to faithfulness than to the accident of physiognomy. "Sara," said Tillat, her voice deep with the promise of surprise, "do you know what *kapura* are?" I was cooking and a little cross. "Of course I do," I answered with some affront. "They're sweetbreads, and they're cooked with kidneys, and they're very good." Natives should always be natives, exactly what they are, and I felt irked to be so probed around the issue of my own nativity. But Tillat's face was kindly with superior knowledge. "Not sweetbread," she gently said. "They're testicles, that's what *kapura* really are." Of course I refused to believe her, went on cooking, and that was the end of that.

The babies left, and I with a sudden spasm of free time watched that organic issue resurface in my head—something that had once sat quite simply inside its own definition was declaring independence from its name and nature, claiming a perplexity that I did not like. And, too, I needed different ways to be still thinking about Tillat, who had gone as completely as she had arrived, and deserved to be reproached for being such an unreliable informant. So, the next time I was in the taut companionship of Pakistanis in New York, I made a point of inquiring into the exact status of *kapura* and the physiological location of its secret, first in the animal and then in the meal. Expatriates are adamant, entirely passionate about such matters as the eating habits of the motherland. Accordingly, even though I was made to feel that it was wrong to strip a food of its sauce and put it back into its bodily belonging, I certainly received an unequivocal response: *kapura*, as naked meat, equals a testicle. Better, it is tantamount to a testicle neatly sliced into halves, just as we make no bones about asking the butcher to split chicken breasts in two. "But," and here I rummaged for the sweet realm of nomenclature, "couldn't *kapura* on a lazy occasion also accommodate something like sweetbreads, which is just a nice way of saying that pancreas is not a pleasant word to eat?" No one, however, was interested in this finesse. "Balls, darling, balls," someone drawled, and I knew I had to let go of the subject.

Yet I was shocked. It was my mother, after all, who had told me that sweetbreads are sweetbreads, and if she were wrong on that score, then how many other simple equations had I now to doubt? The second possibility that occurred to me was even more unsettling: maybe my mother knew that sweetbreads are testicles but had cunningly devised a ruse to make me consume as many parts of the world as she could before she set me loose in it. The thought appalled me. It was almost as bad as attempting to imagine what the slippage was that took me from nipple to bottle and away from the great letdown that signifies lactation. What a falling off! How much I must have suffered when so handed over to the shoddy metaphors of Ostermilk and Babyflo. Gosh, I thought, to think that my mother could do that to me. For of course she must have known, in her Welsh way, that sweetbreads could never be simply sweetbreads in Pakistan. It made me stop and hold my head over that curious possibility: what else have I eaten on her behalf?

I mulled over that question for days, since it wantonly refused to disappear after it had been posed: instead, it settled in my head and insisted on being reformulated, with all the tenacity of a query that actually expects to be met with a reply. My only recourse was to make lists, cramped and strictly alphabetical catalogs of all the gastronomic wrongs I could blame on my mother; but somehow by the time I reached T and "tripe," I was always interrupted and had to begin again. Finally it began to strike me as a rather unseemly activity for one who had always enjoyed a measure of daughterly propriety, and I decided that the game was not to be played again but discarded like table scraps. For a brief span of time I felt free, until some trivial occasion—a dinner, where chicken had been cleverly cooked to resemble veal—caused me to remind my friends of that obsolete little phrase, "mutton dressed up as lamb," which had been such a favorite of my mother's. Another was "neither flesh nor fowl," and as I chatted about the curiousness of those phrases, I suddenly realized that my friends had fallen away and my only audience was the question itself, heaving up its head again and examining me with reproach and some scorn. I sensed that it would be unwise to offer another list to this triumphant interlocutor, so I bowed my head and knew what I had to do. In order to submit even the most imperfect answer, I had to go back to where I belonged and—past a thousand different mealtimes—try to reconstruct the parable of the *kapura*.

Tillat was not around to hear me sigh and wonder where I should possibly begin. The breast would be too flagrant and would make me too tongue-tied, so I decided instead to approach the *kapura* in a mildly devious way, by getting at it through its mate. To the best of my knowledge I had never seen *kapura* cooked outside the company of kidney, and so for Tillat's edification alone I tried to begin with the story of the kidney, which I should have remembered long ago, not twenty-five years after its occurrence. We were living in Lahore, in the 9-T Gulberg house, and in those days our cook was Qayuum. He had a son and two daughters with whom we were occasionally allowed to play: his little girl Munni I specially remember because I liked the way her hair curled and because of all the times that she was such a perfect recipient of fake *pan*. *Pan*, an adult delicacy of betel leaf and nut, can be quite convincingly replicated by a mango leaf stuffed with stones: Ifat, my older sister, would fold such beautifully simulated *pan* triangles that Munni would thrust them into her mouth each time—and then burst into tears. I find it odd today to imagine how that game of guile and trust could have survived even a single repetition, but I recollect it distinctly as a weekly ritual, with us waiting in fascination for Munni to get streetwise, which she never did. Instead, she cried with her mouth wide open and would run off to her mother with little pebbles falling out of her mouth, like someone in a fairy tale.

Those stones get linked to kidneys in my head, as part of the chain through which Munni got the better of me and anticipated the story I really intend to tell. It was an evil day that led her father Qayuum to buy two water buffalo, tether-

24

ing them at the far end of the garden and making my mother beam at the prospect of such fresh milk. My older brother Shahid liked pets and convinced me that we should beam too, until he and I were handed our first overpowering glasses of buffalo milk. Of milks it is certainly the most oceanic, with archipelagoes and gulf streams of cream emitting a pungent, grassy odor. Trebly strong is that smell at milking-time, which my mother beamingly suggested we attend. She kept away herself, of course, so she never saw the big black cows, with their ominous glassy eyes, as they shifted from foot to foot. Qayuum pulled and pulled at their white udders and, in a festive mood, called up the children one by one to squirt a steaming jet of milk into their mouths. When my turn came, my mother, not being there, did not see me run as fast as I could away from the cows and the cook, past the vegetable garden and the goldfish pond, down to the farthermost wall, where I lay down in the grass and tried to faint, but couldn't.

I knew the spot from prior humiliations, I admit. It was where I had hidden twice in the week when I was caught eating cauliflower and was made to eat kidney. The cauliflower came first—it emerged as a fragrant little head in the vegetable garden, a bumpy vegetable brain that looked innocent and edible enough to make me a perfect victim when it called. In that era my greatest illicit joy was hastily chawing off the top of each new cauliflower when no one else was looking. The early morning was my favorite time, because then those flowers felt firm and crisp with dew. I would go to the vegetable patch and squat over the cauliflowers as they came out one by one, hold them between my knees, and chew as many craters as I could into their jaunty tightness. Qayuum was crushed. "There is an animal, Begum Sahib," he mourned to my mother, "like a savage in my garden. *Maro! Maro!*" To hear him made me nervous, so the following morning I tried to deflect attention from the cauliflowers by quickly pulling out all the little radishes while they were still pencil-thin: they lay on the soil like a pathetic accumulation of red herrings. That was when Munni caught me.

"*Abba Ji!*" she screamed for her father like a train engine. Everybody came running, and for a while my squat felt frozen to the ground as I looked up at an overabundance of astonished adult faces. "What are you doing, Sara *Bibi?*" the driver finally and gently asked. "Smelling the radishes," I said in a baby and desperate defiance, "so that the animal can't find the cauliflower." "Which one?" "The new cauliflower." "Which animal, *bibi ji*, you naughty girl?" "The one that likes to eat the cauliflower that I like to smell." And when they laughed at me, I did not know where to put my face for shame.

They caught me out that week, two times over, because after I had been exposed as the cauliflower despoiler and had to enter a new phase of penitence, Qayuum the cook insisted on making me eat kidney. "*Kirrnee,*" he would call it with a glint in his eye, "*kirrnee.*" My mother quite agreed that I should learn such discipline, and the complicated ritual of endurance they imposed did make me teach myself to take a kidney taste without dwelling too long on the peculiarities of kidney texture. I tried to be unsurprised by the mushroom pleats that constitute a kidney's underbelly and by the knot of membrane that holds those kidney folds in place. One day Qayuum insisted that only kidneys could sit on my plate, mimicking legumes and ignoring their thin and bloody juices. Wicked Ifat came into the room and waited till I had started eating; then she intervened. "Sara," said Ifat, her eyes brimming over with wonderful malice, "do you know what kidneys do?" I aged, and my meal regressed, back to its vital belonging in the world of function. "Kidneys make pee, Sara," Ifat told me, "That's what they do, they make pee." And she looked so pleased to be able to tell me that; it made her feel so full of information. Betrayed by food, I let her go, and wept some watery tears into the kidney juice, which was designed anyway to evade cohesion, being thin and in its nature inexact. Then I ran out to the farthermost corner of the garden, where I would later go to hide my shame of milking-time in a retch that refused to materialize.

Born the following year, Tillat would not know that cautionary tale. Nor would she know what Ifat did when my father called from Lady Willingdon Hospital in Lahore to repeat that old phrase, "It is a girl." "It's a girl!" Ifat shouted, as though simply clinching for the world the overwhelming triumph of her will. Shahid, a year my senior, was found half an hour later sobbing next to the goldfish pond near the vegetable garden, for he had been banking on the diluting arrival of a brother. He must have been upset, because when we were taken to visit my mother, he left his penguin—a favorite toy—among the old trees of the hospital garden, where we had been sent to play. I was still uncertain about my relation to the status of this new baby: my sister was glad that it was a girl, and my brother was sad that it wasn't a boy, but we all stood together when penguiny was lost.

It is to my discredit that I forgot this story, both of what the kidney said and what it could have told to my still germinating sister. Had I borne something of those lessons in mind, it would have been less of a shock to have to reconceive the *kapura* parable; perhaps I'd have been prepared for more skepticism about the connection between kidneys and sweetbreads—after all, they fall into no logical category of togetherness. The culinary humor of kidneys and testicles stewing in one another's juices is, on the other hand, very fine: I wish I had had the imagination to intuit all the unwonted jokes people tell when they start cooking food. I should have remembered all those nervously comic edges, and the pangs, that constitute most poignancies of nourishment. And so, as an older mind, I fault myself for not having the wits to recognize what I already knew. I must have always known exactly what *kapura* are, because the conversation they provoked came accompanied with shocks of familiarity that typically attend a trade of solid information. What I had really wanted to reply, first to Tillat and then to my Pakistani friends, was: yes, of course, who do you think I am, what else could they *possibly be?* Anyone with discrimination could immediately discern the connection between *kapura* and their namesake: the shape is right, given that we are now talking about goats; the texture involves a bit of a bounce, which works; and the taste is altogether too exactly what it is. So I should have kept in mind that, alas, we know the flavor of each part of the anatomy: that much imagination belongs to everyone's palate. Once, when my sisters and I were sitting in a sunny winter garden, Tillat began examining some ants that were tumbling about the blades of grass next to her chair. She looked acute and then suddenly said, "How very sour those little ants must be." Ifat declared that she had always thought the same herself, and though I never found out how they arrived at this discovery, I was impressed by it, their ability to take the world on their tongues.

So poor Irfani, how much his infant taste buds must have colored his perception of the grimness of each day. Irfan was born in London, finally another boy, but long after Shahid had ceased looking for playmates in the home. It now strikes me as peculiar that my parents should choose to move back to Pakistan when Farni was barely a year old, and to decide on June, that most pitiless month, in which to return to Lahore. The heat shriveled the baby, giving his face an expression of slow and bewildered shock, which was compounded by the fact that for the next year there was very little that the child could eat. Water boiled ten times over would still retain virulence enough to send his body into derangements, and goat's milk, cow's milk, everything liquid seemed to convey malevolence to his minuscule gut. We used to scour the city for aging jars of imported baby-food; these, at least, he would eat, though with a look of profound mistrust—but even so, he spent most of the next year with his body in violent rebellion against the idea of food. It gave his eyes a gravity they have never lost.

Youngster he was, learning lessons from an infant's intuition to fear food, and to some degree all of us were equally watchful for hidden trickeries in the scheme of nourishment, for the way in which things would always be missing or out of place in Pakistan's erratic emotional market. Items of security—such as flour or butter or cigarettes or tea—were always vanishing, or returning in such dubiously shiny attire that we could barely stand to look at them. We lived in the expectation of threatening surprise: a crow had drowned in the water tank on the roof, so for a week we had been drinking dead-crow water and couldn't understand why we felt so ill; the milkman had accidentally diluted our supply of milk with paraffin instead of water; and those were not pistachios, at all, in a tub of Hico's green ice cream. Our days and our newspapers were equally full of disquieting tales about adulterated foods and the preternaturally keen eye that the nation kept on such promiscuous blendings. I can understand it, the fear that food will not stay discrete but will instead defy our categories of expectation in what can only be described as a manner of extreme belligerence. I like order to a plate, and know the great sense of failure that attends a moment when what is potato to the fork is turnip to the mouth. It's hard, when such things happen.

So, long before the *kapura* made its comeback in my life, we in Pakistan were bedmates with betrayal and learned how to take grim satisfaction from assessing the water table of our outrage. There were both lean times and meaty times, however; occasionally, body and food would sit happily at the same side of the conference table. Take, for example, Ramzan, the Muslim month of fasting, often recollected as the season of perfect meals. Ramzan, a lunar thing, never arrives at the same point of time each year, coming instead with an aura of slight and pleasing dislocation. Somehow it always took us by surprise: new moons are startling to see, even by accident, and Ramzan's moon betokened a month of exquisite precision about the way we were to parcel out our time. On the appointed evenings we would rake the twilight for that possible sliver, and it made the city and body both shudder with expectation to spot that little slip of a moon that signified Ramzan and made the sky historical. How busy

Lahore would get! Its minarets hummed, its municipalities pulled out their old air-raid sirens to make the city noisily cognizant: the moon had been sighted, and the fast begun.

I liked it, the waking up an hour before dawn to eat the prefast meal and chat in whispers. For three wintry seasons I would wake up with Dadi, my grandmother, and Ifat and Shahid: we sat around for hours making jokes in the dark, generating a discourse of unholy comradeship. The food itself, designed to keep the penitent sustained from dawn till dusk, was insistent in its richness and intensity, with bread dripping clarified butter, and curried brains, and cumin eggs, and a peculiarly potent vermicelli, soaked overnight in sugar and fatted milk. And if I liked the getting up at dawn, then Dadi completely adored the eating of it all. I think she fasted only because she so enjoyed the *sehri* meal and that mammoth infusion of food at such an extraordinary hour. At three in the morning the rest of us felt squeamish about linking the deep sleep dreams we had just conducted and so much grease—we asked instead for porridge—but Dadi's eating was a sight to behold and admire. She hooted when the city's sirens sounded to tell us that we should stop eating and that the fast had now begun: she enjoyed a more direct relation with God than did petty municipal authorities and was fond of declaiming what Muhammad himself had said in her defense. He apparently told one of his contemporaries that *sehri* did not end until a white thread of light described the horizon and separated the landscape from the sky. In Dadi's book that thread could open into quite an active loom of dawning: the world made waking sounds, the birds and milkmen all resumed their proper functions, but Dadi's regal mastication—on the last brain now—declared it still was night.

I stopped that early rising years before Tillat and Irfan were old enough to join us, before Ifat ran away to get married, and before my father returned to ritual and overtook his son Shahid's absent place. So my memories of it are scant, the fast of the faithful. But I never lost my affection for the twilight meal, the dusky *iftar* that ended the fast after the mosques had lustily rung with the call for the *maghrib* prayer. We'd start eating dates, of course, in order to mimic Muhammad, but then with what glad eyes we'd welcome the grilled liver and the tang of pepper in the orange juice. We were happy to see the spinach leaves and their fantastical shapes, deftly fried in the lightest chick-pea batter, along with the tenderness of fresh fruit, most touching to the palate. There was a curious invitation about the occasion, converting what began as an act of penance into a godly and obligatory cocktail hour that provided a fine excuse for company and affability. When we lived in Pakistan, that little swerve from severity into celebration happened often. It certainly was true of meatless days.

The country was made in 1947, and shortly thereafter the government decided that two days out of each week would be designated as meatless days, in order to conserve the national supply of goats and cattle. Every Tuesday and Wednesday the butchers' shops would stay firmly closed, without a single carcass dangling from the huge metal hooks that lined the canopies under which the butchers squatted, selling meat, and without the open drains at the side of their narrow street ever running with a trace of blood. On days of normal trade, blood would briskly flow, carrying with it flotillas of chicken feathers, and little bits of sinew and entrail, or a bladder full and yellow that a butcher had just bounced deftly into the drain. On meatless days that world emptied into a skeletal remain: the hot sun came to scorch away all the odors and liquids of slaughter and shriveled on the chopping blocks the last curlicues of anything organic, making them look both vacant and precise.

As a principle of hygiene I suppose it was a good idea although it really had very little to do with conservation: the people who could afford to buy meat, after all, were those who could afford refrigeration, so the only thing the government accomplished was to make some people's Mondays very busy indeed. The Begums had to remember to give the cooks thrice as much money; the butchers had to produce thrice as much meat; the cooks had to buy enough flesh and fowl and other sundry organs to keep an averagely carnivorous household eating for three days. A favorite meatless day breakfast, for example, consisted of goat's head and feet cooked with spices into a rich and ungual sauce—remarkable, the things that people eat. And so, instead of creating an atmosphere of abstention in the city, the institution of meatless days rapidly came to signify the imperative behind the acquisition of all things fleshly. We thought about beef, which is called "big meat," and we thought about mutton, "little meat," and then we collectively thought about chicken, the most coveted of them all.

But here I must forget my American sojourn, which has taught me to look on chicken as a notably undignified bird, with pimply skin and pockets of fat tucked into peculiar places and unnecessarily meaty breasts. Those meatless day fowls, on the other hand, were a thing apart. Small, not much bigger than the average quail, they had a skin that cooked to the texture of rice paper, breaking even over the most fragrant limbs and wings. Naturally we cherished them and lavished much care on trying to obtain the freshest of the crop. Once I was in Karachi with my sister Nuz when the thought that she had to engage in the social ferocity of buying chickens was making her quite depressed. We went anyway, with Nuz assuming an alacrity that had nothing to do with efficiency and everything to do with desperation. Nuz stood small and dark in the chicken-monger's shop, ordered her birds, paid for them, and then suddenly remembered her housewifely duty. "Are they fresh?" she squawked, clutching at them, "Can you promise me they're fresh?" The chicken-monger looked at her with some perplexity. "But Begum Sahib," he said gently, "they're alive."

"Oh," said Nuz, "so they are," and calmed down immediately. I have always admired her capacity to be reassured by the world and take without a jot of embarrassment any comfort it is prepared to offer. So I thought she had forgotten about the issue of freshness as we drove home (with the dejected chickens tied up in a rope basket on the back seat) and the Karachi traffic grew lunchtime crazed. But "Oh," she said again, half an hour later, "So a fresh chicken is a dead chicken." "Not too dead," I replied. It made us think of meatless days as some vast funeral game, where Monday's frenetic creation of fresh things beckoned in the burial meals of Tuesday and Wednesday. "Food," Nuz said with disgust— "It's what you bury in your body." To make her feel less alone, we stopped at Shezan's on the way home, to get her an adequate supply of marzipan; for she eats nothing but sweet things. Food she'll cook—wonderful *Sindi* tastes, exotic to my palate—but sugar is the only thing Nuz actually wants to taste.

Irfan was the same about birds. He preferred to grow them rather than eat them. There was a time when he had a hundred doves on the roof of the Khurshid Alam Road house, which was quite a feat, considering that they'd had to be kept a strict secret from my father. Papa hated doves, associating them with the effete gambling of Deccan princedoms or with Trafalgar Square and his great distaste of the English ability to combine rain and pigeon droppings. So Irfan built dovecote after dovecote on our roof, while Papa had no idea of the commerce and exchange beneath which he was living. When he stayed at home to write, every sound would send him snarling, so then he heard with passionate hatred the long and low dove murmurings. He groaned and pulled his hair to think that his rooftop could actually be hospitable to pigeons: every evening he would dispatch Irfan to stand on the flat brick roof that was designed for summer sleep beneath the stars, so that he could shoo the birds away before they even dreamed of cooing. Since twilight was the hour when Farni preferred to feed the doves, life between him and Papa was perfect for a while. But then things fell apart. One afternoon Papa suddenly remembered that Irfan was at school and felt it incumbent on himself to gather as much information as he could about the academic progress of his youngest child, the renegade. In the evenings two tutors would come to coach Irfan in Urdu and math, and to them my father turned for an assessment of his son. "Too unhappy!" wailed the math master, "Today just too sad!" Papa bridled with defensiveness, asking for more specific fact. "Cat, sir, cat," mourned the Urdu teacher, "Cat has eaten up his fifty doves." The math master shook his head in commiseration, and Papa later liked to claim that his mind went from "bats in the belfry" through every possible idiomatic permutation he could give to cats and doves, until— only just realizing he had heard a literal truth—he stared from one face to the next, like a man aghast with knowledge.

Am I wrong, then, to say that my parable has to do with nothing less than the imaginative extravagance of food and all the transmogrifications of which it is capable? Food certainly gave us a way not simply of ordering a week or a day but of living inside history, measuring everything we remembered against a chronology of cooks. Just as Papa had his own yardstick—a word he loved—with which to measure history and would talk about the Ayub era, or the second martial law, or the Bhutto regime, so my sisters and I would place ourselves in time by remembering and naming cooks. "In the Qayuum days," we'd say, to give a distinctive flavor to a particular anecdote, or "in the Allah Ditta era." And our evocations only get more passionate now that cooks are a dying breed in Pakistan and have left us for the more ample kitchens of the gulf states and the more cramped but lucrative spaces of the Curries in a Hurry at Manchester and Leeds. There is something nourishing about the memory of all those shadow dynasties: we do not have to subsist only on the litany that begins, "After General Ayub came General Yahya; after the Bhutto years came General Zulu Haq," but can also add; "Qayuum begat Shorty and his wife; and they begat the Punjabi poet only called Khansama; he begat Ramzan and Karam Dad the bearer; Ramzan begat Tassi-Passi, and he begat Allah Ditta, meanest of them all."

We were always waiting for Allah Ditta to die. He was a

good cook and a mean man who announced the imminence of his death for years, though he ended up surviving nearly half of the family. Still, he was useful. My mother was a nervous cook—probably because her mother had been a stern woman about such decorum—and was glad to be able to turn everything over to Allah Ditta and take refuge instead in the university. It is odd to recall that her precise mind could see a kitchen as an empty space; I think she had given suck so many times and had engaged in so many umbilical connections that eating had become syncopated in her head to that miraculous shorthand. Not that pregnancy was a mystical term in her lexicon: on the contrary, the idea would make her assume a fastidious and pained expression. So she absolutely understood when Ifat, large with Ayesha this time, wafted into the house and murmured, "Do you know what it is like to have something kicking at you all the time and realize that you can never kick it back?" Mamma, never one to state the obvious, would look up pleadingly at that, as though the obvious was so much with us anyway that we all deserved to be spared its articulation. Or she would utter one of her curious archaisms: "Don't fret, child," she'd say, "don't fret."

But Ifat was good at fretting, apt at creating an aura of comfort by being able to characterize precisely the details of anything that could be discomforting to her. And so the state of pregnancy could on occasion make her eyes abstract, as she looked down at herself and vaguely said, "I've eaten too much, I've eaten too much." "There's too much body about the business," she once told me, "and too much of it is your own." Later, when Ayesha was born, a girl with blue unfurling fingers, the baby still would not permit my sister to empty into peace. She refused to eat enough, bloating her mother's breasts into helpless engorgement. So Ifat lay in bed, surrounded by such instruments of torture as breast pumps and expressers and her great facility for imprecation. Expressing letters rather than breasts was my normal ken, and it hurt to watch the meticulousness with which she set about relieving her body of that extraneous liquid. It was worse than a dentist, and for hours we implored her to take respite, but Ifat would not stop until her ferocious fever turned to sweat and her face was as white as in labor. Then she slept, waking once out of a dream like a beautiful gaunt owl to look at me oddly and say, "Mamma fed me once." In the morning the infant ate, and when Ifat's breasts lost their raging heat, it was as though stiffness could leave the entire household, erect as we had been to her distress. "Ordinary pumps again," she breathed, "they're mine again, at last." We smiled at that. Hard to believe, today, that those machines are gone for good.

For Ifat always was a fine source of stories about the peculiarities of food, particularly on the points of congruence between the condition of pregnancy and the circumstance of cooking, since both teeter precariously between the anxieties of being overdone and being underdone. When I left Pakistan, I had to learn how to cook—or, better—how to conceive of a kitchen as a place where I actually could be private. Now I like to cook, although I remain fascinated by my deep-seated inability to boil an egg exactly to the point that I would like to see it boiled, which seems like such an easy accomplishment of the efficient. I have finally come to the realization that I must feel slightly peculiar about eggs, because I am uneasy until they have been opened up and the flagrant separation between yolk and egg can be whisked into some yellow harmony. When I simply try to boil an egg, I've noticed, I am sure to give it an unconsciously advertent crack, so that the humming water suddenly swirls with something viscous, and then I have to eat my eggs with gills and frills. Not that I very frequently boil an egg: once in five years, perhaps. I can distinctly remember the last occasion: it was when I was about to be visited by the tallest man in my acquaintance, in the days when I still used to tolerate such things.

He was a curious chap, whose bodily discomfort with the world was most frequently expressed in two refrains: one was "Not enough food!" and the second, "Too much food!" During the era of our association, I rapidly learned that the one intimacy we had to eschew above all others was the act of making meals and eating them alone. We could eat in restaurants and public places, surrounded by the buffer of other tables and strangers' voices, but for the two of us to be making and taking a meal on our own was such a fearful thought that the physical largess at my side would break into a myriad of tiny quakes. It was revelatory for me, who had never before watched someone for whom a dining table was so markedly more of a loaded domestic space than was a bed, but I was not totally averse to this new logic. It exercised my imagination to devise oblique methods of introducing food into my house, free-floating and aimless items that could find their way into anyone's mouth with such studied carelessness that they could do no damage to the integrity of a flea. I felt as though I were still in Sussex, putting out a saucer of milk and goodwill for the hedgehogs in the garden and then discreetly vanishing before they froze into prickles of shyness and self-dismay. "What is it, after all, between food and the body?" I asked one day in an exasperation of pain, and never got an answer in reply.

Tom and Tillat tried to behave like friends; they cooked together in a way I liked—but with me the man was so large that he could conceive of himself only in bits, always conscious of how segments of his body could go wandering off, tarsals and metatarsals heedlessly autonomous. Such dissipation made him single-minded. He never worried about the top of his head, because he had put it behind him. His mother chose his glasses for him. His desires made him merely material: he looked at himself just as a woman looks when her infant takes its first tremulous step into the upright world, melting her into a modesty of consternation and pride. And his left hand could never see what his right hand was doing, for they were too far apart, occupying as they did remote hemispheres of control. Perhaps I should have been able to bring those bits together, but such a narrative was not available to me, not after what I knew of storytelling. Instead, we watched the twist through which food became our staple metaphor, suggesting that something of the entire event had—against our will—to do with hunger. "You do not have the backbone of a shrimp," I mourned, gazing up at the spread-sheet of that man mountain. "You have a head the size of a bowl of porridge and a brain the size of a pea." This was in a restaurant. I was surprised beyond measure when that big head bent back and wept, a quick summer shower of tears. By the time he left, all surfaces were absolutely dry.

In any event, rain in America has never felt to me like a condition of glad necessity, and Tom and I will never know the conversations that we might have had on something like the twelfth of August in Lahore, for nothing can approximate what the monsoons make available in happy possibility. I think it was the smell that so intoxicated us after those dreary months of nostril-scorching heat, the smell of dust hissing at the touch of rain and then settling down, damply placid on the ground. People could think of eating again: after the first rains, in July, they gave themselves over to a study of mangoes, savoring in high seriousness the hundred varieties of that fruit. When it rained in the afternoons, children were allowed to eat their mangoes in the garden, stripped naked and dancing about, first getting sticky with mango juice and then getting slippery with rain. In our time such games drove Ifat and Shahid and me quite manic in our merriment, while Mamma sat reading on a nearby monsoon veranda to censor us if we transgressed too far. Years later, Tillat and I served a similar function when Ifat left her children with us—we sat on the veranda, letting them play in the rain. Ifat would have rushed off to shop or to do something equally important, while her children would long for Irfan, whom they loved boisterously, to come back from school. Mamma, on such afternoons, would not be there. It returns as a poignancy to me, that I have forgotten where Mamma could possibly be on such an occasion.

She was not there on the afternoon when, after the rains had whetted our appetites, I went out with my old friends

Nuzhat Ahmad and Ayla, as the three of us often did, in a comradeship of girlhood. We went driving to Bagh-e-Jinnah, formerly known as Lawrence Gardens, located opposite the Governor's House along the Mall in Lahore. We were trying to locate the best *gol guppa* vendor in town and stopped by to test the new stand in Lawrence Gardens. *Gol guppas* are a strange food: I have never located an equivalent to them or their culinary situation. They are an outdoor food, a passing whim, and no one would dream of recreating their frivolity inside her own kitchen. A *gol guppa* is a small hollow oval of the lightest pastry that is dipped into a fiery liquid sauce made of tamarind and cayenne and lemon and cold water. It is evidently a food invented as a joke, in a moment of good humor. We stopped the car next to some tall jaman trees (which many years before Shahid and I loved to climb) and enjoyed ourselves a great deal, until a friendly elbow knocked the bowl of *gol guppa* sauce all over my lap. It gave me a new respect for foodstuffs, for never has desire brought me to quite such an instantaneous effect. My groin's surprise called attention to passageways that as a rule I am only theoretically aware of owning, all of which folded up like a concertina in protest against such an explosive aeration. For days after, my pupils stayed dilated, while my interiors felt gaunt and hollow-eyed.

I retold this ten-year-old episode to Tillat when she came visiting, shortly after she had hit me over the head with her testicles-equal-*kapura* tale. I was trying to cheer her up and distract her from the rather obvious fact that, once again, her children were refusing to eat. "Do you know how much happier my life would be if my children would eat?" Tillat wailed, and there was little I could say to deny it. "It's your fault, Tatty," I said consolingly, "your body manufactured chocolate milk." Certainly those children had a powerful impulse toward chocolate: it was deranging, to pull out the Cadbury's for breakfast. It gave Tillat a rather peculiar relation to food: it made her a good cook but a somewhat stern one, as though she were always waiting for her meals to undergo a certain neurotic collapse. One day she turned quite tragic, cooking for some visitors of mine, when the *shami kebabs* she was frying obstinately refused to cohere into their traditional shape. I did not expect Tillat's moon-face to look so wracked, as though the secret of all things lay in that which made the *shami* cling to the *kebab*. "Never mind, Tillat. We'll just call them Kuwaiti *kebabs* and then no one will know they look peculiar." Of course I was right, and the meal was most satisfactory.

I missed Tillat's children when they left. There are too many of them, of course—all of my siblings have had too many. Each year I resolve afresh that my quota of aunthood is full, that I no longer am going to clutter my head with new names, new birthdays. But then something happens, like finding in the mail another photograph of a new baby, and against my will they draw me in again. I did not see Ifat's children for four years after she had died, and when Tillat and I visited them in Rawalpindi, in the pink house on the hill, Ayesha, the youngest, whispered to her paternal grand-mother, "My aunts smell like my mother." When she repeated that to me, it made me tired and grave. Tillat and I slept for ten hours that night, drowning in a sleep we could not forestall, attempting to waken and then falling back exhausted into another dreamless hour.

I described that sleep to Shahid, wondering about it, during one of our rare encounters. I was trying to imagine what it would be like not to meet his children again, since in those days he had lost them. We talked about that, he and I, walking through the benign winter of a London after-noon, while the light was failing in irregular slashes. I always feel quiet to be walking at his side, glad to notice all the ways his face has taken age and yet remains the same. That face and I occupied the same playpen, ate sand out of the same sandbox together. I had not seen him for two years, which made me tender when we met, talking about how we could not see Surraya and Karim, his children. "I'll tell you what it's like, Sara," Shahid said. Then he stopped still and looked at me. "It's like the thing that a lush forgets, which is the absence of extremity."

All at once I felt relieved my mother was not there to overhear such conversation. I was glad that I had never seen, could no longer see, the cast her face would surely have taken hearing that sentence from her son. I wanted her to be put where she should be put, away from all of this, back in a bed where she need not have to know the desperate sleep Tillat and I had slept, hour after hour of reaching for the shoreline only to be pulled back into unending night. It was almost her reproach that I wished to be spared, the quiet voice that would look up and say, "Honestly, you children." I was afraid she would tell us that we were just as careless with our children as we had been with our books or our toys or our clothes, and I did not want to hear her proven right. The chagrin of the thought perplexed me as Shahid and I walked on, until I suddenly remembered the chagrin on Barkat the washerman's face when he was three days late in bringing back our school uniforms. Mamma's Urdu was an erratic thing, with sudden moments of access into idioms whose implications would throw her audience into gasps of surprise. When Barkat's recalcitrance kept her children denuded of clean white starched shirts and dresses to wear to school each day, Mamma's Urdu took a deep breath and opened the nearest idiomatic door, which sent her unknowing into the great precisions of classic amorous discourse. Barkat did not know where to look in his chagrin when Mamma gazed at him and said, her reproach as clear as a bell, "Barkat, how could you cause me such exquisite pain?" I reminded Shahid of that story. It made us laugh from Connaught Court to Edgware Road.

Tillat has three children, none of whom my mother ever saw, and I missed them after they left New Haven. I could not forget the way Tillat's three-year-old and only daughter, called Heba, broke my heart when she refused to swallow food. She sat at a table putting food in her mouth and growing chipmunk cheeks: we would try to ignore them as long as we could, but Heba knew how nervous we were getting, that we would soon break down and let her spit her mouthfuls out, whereupon she could resume her lovely jabber as though no grief had transpired at all. She ravaged me, but somehow it was consoling to be so readily available to pain and to observe in her manner and her face some ancient lineaments of my own. One day she startled me by confidentially saying that her brother Omi has a penis, but she has blood. When I asked her what she meant, "I looked inside to see," she answered, and glanced at me pragmatically. It made me glad for her that she had had such introspective courage to knock at the door of her body and insist it let her in. Heba has large eyes, as black as grapes, and hands that she wields like an Indian dancer. "Why don't you like me, Omi?" she would ask relentlessly. "I'm nice, too." It drove her elder brother into furies of rage. "I don't like you! I don't!" Omi shouted, while Heba looked at him with curiosity. Watching over her baby patience, I realized I need not worry about her, that child who was busy adding herself to the world and would not rest until it had made her properly welcome, long after she had forgotten me.

It reminds me that I am glad to have washed my hands of my sister Ifat's death and can think of her now as a house I once rented but which is presently inhabited by people I do not know. I miss her body, of course, and how tall she was, with the skull of a leopard and the manner of a hawk. But that's aesthetic, and aside from it, Ifat is just a repository of anecdotes for me, something I carry around without noticing, like lymph. One morning last year I woke myself up at dawn to escape the involutions of a dream that held me like a tax collector in a place where I did not want to be. For a moment I could not remember what city I was in, or what bedroom, until everything became lucid as I realized that Ifat was dead at last. "Darling, what a nosebleed," I found myself saying before I slept again and paid my dues.

Thus Nuz was right, absolutely right, when she wrote to me in her sprawling handwriting that looks so much like Karachi and said indignantly, "Of course my hair is going to fall out, what do you expect, when life is so full of stress? Now I wear a wig and look smarter than ever." Then she added, with the uncanny knowledge only Nuz can muster, "People are only good for light conversation." I liked the way that phrase lingered, born as it was from Nuzzi's unwitting capacity for the lingering phrase. The last time I was in London, I never saw Shahid's face light up so brightly as when he showed me a card that read, in florid script, "Greetings from Pakistan," beneath the image of some bustling Pathan dancers. Inside it Nuz had written, "Dearest Shahid, I am so sorry to hear of your divorce, my mother has had a brain hemorrhage and I am completely shattered, Merry Christmas and Happy New Year. Love, Nuz." Nuzzi's mother was my father's first wife, and also his cousin, so I suppose she can count as a relative of ours although we have never met. Luckily she made a miraculous recovery before Nuz went completely bald.

My own mother would hate it that we could laugh at such a tale. Such merriment made her look at her progeny with suspicion, unable to accept that she could ever whelp this mordant laughter. When Ifat was pregnant with Alia, I remember how worried Mamma looked one day when she came across Ifat's first child, little Tunsi-boy, telling his nurse that Ama had eaten another baby so he'd have a brother or a sister soon. "So they think you eat them up!" I was full of exclamation when Ifat told me this story, which made us laugh in poignant glee. Mamma came into the room and looked at us in a growing recognition of dismay. "Perhaps you do," she quietly said.

Five years later, I wish I had understood and remembered my mother's reprimand during the week she finally died. Sitting in the American Midwest, I thought of all my brothers and sisters, who watched my mother die in the jaunty dawn of a March day and who—fatigued and uncaring of the delicious respite of the dateline—gave me eight hours when Mamma was still historically alive. In a Lahore dawn on the ninth of March my mother's body failed to register on the hospital's gray screens; I in America was informed on the eighth, so technically I had a few more hours of my mother's life to savor before I needed to consign her into the ground. It made me secretly angry that such a reticent woman could choose to do something so rash and declarative as to die in such a double-handed way.

And then, when I was trying to move away from the raw irritability of grief, I dreamed a dream that left me reeling. It put me in London, on the pavement of some unlovely street, an attempted crescent of vagrant houses. A blue van drove up: I noticed it was a refrigerated car and my father was inside it. He came to tell me that we must put my mother in her coffin, and he opened the blue hatch of the van to make me reach inside, where it was very cold. What I found were hunks of meat wrapped in cellophane, and each of them felt like Mamma, in some odd way. It was my task to carry those flanks across the street and to fit them into the coffin at the other side of the road, like pieces in a jigsaw puzzle. Although my dream will not let me recall how many trips I made, I know my hands felt cold. Then, when my father's back was turned, I found myself engaged in rapid theft—for the sake of Ifat and Shahid and Tillat and all of us, I stole away a portion of that body. It was a piece of her foot I found, a small bone like a knuckle, which I quickly hid inside my mouth, under my tongue. Then I and the dream dissolved, into an extremity of tenderness.

It is hard to believe today that I thought the dream too harsh a thing. As parable, the *kapura* does not dare to look much further. It wishes to take the taste of my imagination only quite so far and, like my mother, makes me trebly entranced; had I really been perplexed at such a simple thing? Or perhaps my mind had designed me to feel rudely tender. I had eaten, that was all, and woken to a world of meatless days.

# MUSTAKORI, MY FRIEND:
# A STUDY OF
# PERFECT IGNORANCE

Known severally in her Western manifestations as Congo Lise, Fancy Musgrave, and Faze Mackaw, Mustakor of Tanzania is a woman to amaze her coterie of friends. Small, and of slavish disposition, she is never happier than when bustling her energies to the betterment of someone else. In how many cities and on how many afternoons have we watched her darken the light by nipping in and out of our attention spans for a quick good deed! On days when the mind is most concerned with maintaining an untrammeled lethargy, then Mustakori is bound to arrive, washing windows, emptying ashtrays, chirpily hammering a nail askew in a bookshelf long past repair. It hurts, of course, the perpetual annoyance of her goodness. But still that's not what so amazes us.

The surprise of Mustakor constitutes the subject of this story, and I invite all of you to join me in a posture of communal flabbergastion, so that we jointly understand how soothing it can be to point our accusations at her each time existence generates some fresh ineptitude. It is a relief with which I am long familiar: during the two decades of our comradeship I learned early to look upon Congo Lise as the root, the etymology, of irritation, so that any great annoyance of spirit still makes me scream out, "Mustakor!" The only trouble with this talisman is that it has two little feet that come panting over at the vaguest glimmerings of a bidding, for every cry of wolf sets Mustakori running, and she will not see the moral written, not in her lifetime.

I was talking about it to Dale the other day, Dale of the pallid cheekbones, who is often disturbed by my propensity to take her name in vain. It is hardly surprising, however, that she should function in my head as such a habit of refrain, for we have been in conversation now for the last ten years and have never yet brought to conclusion any one of the things we started to say. (So though I know that you're here against your will and that I should not detain you, please listen to my promise, Dale: if you will stay now, within the privacy of parentheses, then I'll not again disturb the ways you are invisible between us. So stay, be gray-eyed among these sentences for a brief time, and then you can go for good.) In our early years, those most intensely talkable, Dale and I so savored the taste of articulating ourselves in each other's presence that we rarely conversed outside the splendid way a life unfolds itself to its most prized audience. Now, however, we are more discreet: our landscapes are worn, full of old and nubbly mountains, less interested in the great continental shift that hefted us into being in the first place than in the ordinary accident of things, the lope of a passing camel or the strut of a goat. Today, we rarely—gingerly— talk about ourselves. But we still talk about Mustakor.

"She really is amazing, because," said Dale, unconsciously imitating her daughter's erstwhile habit of uttering an uplifted "because" every time she really wanted to begin a sentence with a more punchy "why." "I have to go to bed now," Zoë at three would say, "because?" I'd feel guilty when I ignored that delicate punctuation, which I did, in the lazy corner-cutting style that pretends it is too adult to hear precisely the locutions of a child. On the subject of Mustakor, however, I was not prepared to let a single dog stay sleeping on the ground. "Because" I pronounced, scowling at a nearby cigarette, "she was born stupid and will die stupid. And that's the end of that." Then, through the silence at the other end of the line—for, now that we rarely meet, I think we have learned to graph each other's voices on the telephone— I saw Dale imply that, in fact, what I'd said was only a beginning, but it would do as a roughshod start.

What then are my options? I suppose I could recall that I first met Mustakori in college, at Kinnaird, but then what a Jonah my voice feels to the whale of that context. It makes mind and body boggle: Kinnaird College! for Women! on Jail Road! in Lahore! A place to imprint on unsuspecting faces looks of indelible surprise! The college was indeed on Jail Road, as was the jail, and the racecourse, and the lunatic asylum, too: daily we found it hard to believe ourselves, but it was true. All those institutions looked identical, built out of the same colonial red brick in a style that suggested a profusion of archways and verandas and enclosed gardens, highly walled. Massive thrice-locked gates dotted that potent street, which the city vainly tried to rename, but Jail Road—a simple and accurate appellation—refused any alias.

I was the third of Papa's daughters to be sent to Kinnaird. Miss Robinson was principal when I joined: Nuzzi and Ifat had preceded me during the Miss Mangat Rai era, while Tillat was to follow, after us all, in the days of Mira Phailbus herself. When I was at Kinnaird, Mira was still a lecturer, contemporary of Perin Cooper, the Zoroastrian drama teacher who was famous for a body like a bird and a minuscule ribcage in which, everyone knew, sat two tigers' worth of theatrical aplomb. In that era, theater and Kinnaird sat cheek by jowl in the imagination of Lahore, superficially because of its dramatic societies and annual plays, more significantly because of the histrionic terror engendered by its secret locked-up space. To the city, after all, Kinnaird signified a magical arena containing a few hundred women of prime-time marriageability in an architectural embrace remarkably reminiscent of the old days of the *zenana khana*, its room after room of unenterable women's rooms. And we who lived on the inside of that idea were caught in that curiously constricting position: we felt imprisoned in the very place we knew represented an area of rampant fantasy in the city's psychic life. It made us a trifle sad, I think, to have to wake and sleep to the rhythm of being perpetually wanted, like having to cover up for the frequent mundanity of dawns. Some women insisted that they loved it, glad to barter the actual boredom of our daily doings for the glamour of some third-person daydream. And others, little Perin Cooper included, felt daunted and jittery at the prospect of trying to stay real amid the perpetual onslaught of unreality. Which was more real: we, Kinnaird, on the inside—or the little bits of fantastic longing that drove their traffic outside and around our walls? We never really knew what we tried to ask, but we felt the twinge of it as a failure of lucidity. Were we in or out? Odd, the indeterminacy we managed to create about where the spectacle actually was that all of us were watching.

The hostels where the boarders slept (Jubilee, A-Hostel, B-Hostel, and so forth, with B-Hostel sunny-side housing the most sought-after quarters) were intended by college rule never to be entered by a man, other than at best a father or at worst a sweeper. Rumor had it, however, that certain hair-raising challenges had been met by the bravest and most depraved of the boarders, who then had entertained all kinds of nocturnal possibilities. When I first joined Kinnaird, they told me that my sister Ifat had been on the inside of that dark freemasonry, but since I had arrived in the wake of her flamboyant runaway marriage, I soon got used to seeing the college conjure her up as the swashbuckling brigand in all kinds of unlikely scenarios. As a consequence, her scandal sat upon me like a crown, and I was swathed about in little bits and pieces of Ifat-gossip, in her rags and bones. It took me a while to understand the true theater of it all—that I was never allowed to be part of Ifat's audience but instead was supposed to be her again, trotted out by popular demand for an easy replay. Kinnaird was disgusted when I said no, and regarded me as though my aura held at least as much aggravation as that surrounding an unwashed peach. But Ifat is a tale unto herself, not a fruit in someone else's basket, as she would be the first to claim. "Am I," she suggests in spirit, "as simple as an analogy?" Part of me wishes she would answer the question for herself before she goes away, but tonight Ifat is long past summoning. "Go back to Mowgli!"—Ifat's name for Mustakor—"Write your Jungle Book!" This evening she is a disheveled and indignant ghost.

So oh, poor Mowgli! What must it have been like to lope into Lahore fresh from East Africa and then, let alone Lahore, to lope into Kinnaird! She came with all the tentative innocence of one who returns, seeking to understand the geographic reality of her forebears and waiting to locate in an unknown mode of speech the wraith of an intuitively familiar cadence. Those who travel curiously imagine that returning is somehow sweeter, less dangerous, than seeking out some novel history, and Mustakor evidently had such nostalgia encoded in her genes. Of course, she was disappointed in Lahore, arriving as she did like an eager pony and finding in place of welcome a deep historical dislike, which placed her cheek to cheek with the term "brown European," another name to vex her need of equanimity. Given the names she had collected on prior continents, I was amazed to see how many cheeks Mustakori found it in herself to turn within a given day; ultimately, it was her commitment to innocence that flabbergasted me. Perin Cooper noted the same. She gazed at her for half a day, narrowing her eyes when Mustakor straggled across campus, her body fretting against its own need for physical ease. "What I saw," Perin later announced, "was an actress, and an actress is what we need." I was impressed by that, both by the accuracy of her eye and the reticence of her remark. For what little Perin Cooper had really detected in Mustakori's desperate lolls was her deep allegiance to the principle of radical separation: mind and body, existence and performance, would never be allowed to occupy the same space of time. And since Mustakor could not let herself understand the principle of double occupancy, Perin Cooper decided to make full use of such pristine single-mindedness. She cast her as the tramp in *The Insect Play*, and everyone loved to watch Fancy Musgrave unleashing her sorrowful range of monkey expressions, playing in our midst the part of the outside.

How earnestly she went at it. It was curious to watch her literally believe that acting was a reality, an activity as tangible as high-jump, in which once the pole had been finally sent clattering into the sand, one just stopped jumping and went away. Mustakori's ability for desperate concentration always amazed Perin Cooper, who did not anticipate such a blind fidelity to the task immediately at hand. Could Mustakor not notice that any self-respecting task is bound to develop a bout of shifty jitters when subjected to an overly faithful hand? What dimly recollected event had taught her to conceive of desperation as a synonym of devotion? Many have asked that question, many times. Recently, at a conference entitled "The Eastern Woman in the Western World: Gender, Race, Ideology," I came across several subgroups of Mustakori's friends, and was astonished to see how much agreement she could generate among a disparate group of people. "It's not that I resent goodwill," blushed a puzzled Englishman, "but why should it turn the erotic litmus blue when I'd much rather it be red?" "School," scowled Zoreen, "Mustakori can't leave school." Then she slouched out, redmouthed. Later, at the cash bar, I found myself in conversation with a skinny Mexican, discussant for a panel that I'd missed. "Mustakor?" he said, "Ya Mustakor, ya Mustakor!" and danced some twirling steps. "Her mind is birjin," he told me conspiratorially, "as birjin as a pile of driven snow." He smiled moistly at that and left me to ponder on virginity, completely on my own.

David was not at the conference, though I had hoped to see him there, which is hardly surprising, since after all these years it has become a tiny habit of my soul to hope to bump into David. We had known him, Faze Mackaw and I, when he was directing an Urdu program in Lahore for an American university. For us, he immediately registered as one of those rare Americans whose seduction at the hands of the subcontinent remained all the more complete because it was unglamourous—there is nothing that can disappoint someone who has learned to be engaged by the wavering course of disappointment! David sat like a cartographer, trying to teach his perplexed group of students how to teach themselves by simply living in the city of Lahore, and learning himself— how urgent those sunny mornings felt—to be our friend. He was given living quarters high up in Ewing Hall, a sprawling edifice that lay adjacent to the old campus of Punjab University, which, built in the latter day of the British raj, links in hysteric abundance the Victorian style with cupola and dome. There, in the thick white-walled and high-ceilinged peace of Ewing Hall, I'd sit each morning with David and our friend Mustakor, living for a few hours off conversation and contraband coffee, smuggled from India, never openly available in Pakistan. It was David who first suggested to me that Mustakori's amazement could be assessed only by a geographic computation. "Simply count the places," he said, and looked meaningful. But when I repeated the conversation to Mustakori, she only seemed crushed at the vision of a discourse that actually conceived of her in the third person. It made her shudder, such a primal scene. "Do it, then," she said, with the bustling concern of a nervous cockatoo, "compute." And so I did.

The first place where she lived was East Africa. My most trustworthy sources intimate that Mustakori was born in the early 1950s, in the Tanganyika that was, the Tanzania of today. Her birthplace was Arusha, coffee-growing girdle of a district, lying in the shadow of Mount Meru: a mountain, they say, which is far more shapely and satisfactory qua mountain than Kilimanjaro's inflated slopes. Her parents, Asiatics, claimed origin from the Indian Punjab and Kashmir, via a detour through Hong Kong, but I cannot stop to explain that complex wrinkle. Mustakor ended up in Dublin when she was two years old, living with a relative who held

51

the dubious distinction of being the first Indian in Ireland to put *salan* into cans and market it under the inventive brand name, "Curry in a Hurry". In later years it could cause me a moment of embarrassed astonishment to hear the zest with which Mustakori made public such easily hidden family secrets. After Ireland she was sent to English boarding schools for girls, places that wrung the Swahili out of her insides, leaving instead a single-minded need to remain faithful to her idea of home as a solitary mountain rising very exactly out of East African terrain. Terrible, the way those schools deforested the lingo of our girl, so that when she most seriously wished to grope for the shadow of a perfect mountain, all she could find of her voice was its fault. Late at night, after hostel lights were out, she lay insomniac in bed, trying to image Meru. It was super. Very ripping. Jolly good.

After Devon came Kenya, the Loreto Convent High School (for girls), an institution that sat on the outskirts of Nairobi and greatly prided itself on the sweeping curve of its bougainvillea-lined drive. But a fire came one night, burning down those great purple bushes and sending Sister Annunciata's normal demeanor into a manic passion of dismay. She ran up and down the driveway all night, urging the firemen on in a voice that the girls had never heard before: the students watched from their windows in a silent chorus and in the morning discovered that the bushes had vanished into heaps of charred and dank stumps and that Sister Annunciata had died in her sleep. Anyone who has served time in a convent school can proffer an equivalent anecdote, or walks about with a similar nun story in her head. But Mustakor was less traumatized by the nuns than she was by being the first Asian student in that most colonial school. It bred in her a dislike for postindependence Kenya and its all-too-happy meld of East and West, making Nairobi such a continuingly temperate city for Europeans. The temperate was obviously not her cup of tea, despite the slopes of Devon: no, anyone with a temperate hankering would not suddenly quit Kenya for seven years (poor Mustakor!) of Pakistan without parole. "Too much curry, not enough hurry," as Shahid sympathetically said.

So there is Mustakor, *hodi*-ing at the edge of my memory, trying to get into Pakistan. *Hodi*, the African greeting ("Is anyone at home? Can I come in?"), constitutes a major portion of my friend Mustakor's Swahili vocabulary: consequently, I want to do it justice and give it the eminence it deserves. "*Hodi*," said Mustakor, a little meekly, to the immigrations official at the half-built and already squalid customs building at Karachi Airport. It made him look at her suspiciously, but nonetheless he stamped her blue D-status British passport, and Mustakor's fate was sealed. At that point in time—two summers before the 1971 war—I was in all likelihood circling the city of Lahore in a little Cessna two-seater, having a serious conversation with Tarik Khan. Tarik (T.K., as his male friends called him, saying "*Yar*, that T.K., he's a bloody good chap!") had a passion for little airplanes and for me, and each time he wanted to have a serious conversation, we would solemnly go to Walton Airport in Lahore, get into his little Cessna, and then circle the city, waiting for talk to descend on us. That it rarely did was hardly our fault: the Cessna was noisy, and Lahore in June can be hot, even at sky level. I who loved the jut of his lower lip was quite content to be up there in silence, sweating in an illicit sky, and watching my friend T.K. formulate and reformulate sentences I knew he would never say. Down on the ground there was too much chatter anyway, so it established a poignancy of comradeship between us, all that machinery and silence. Only once he startled me out of equanimity by suddenly saying, "But why?" proving that there is something after all to old wives' tales of mind reading, lipreading. "I do love your mouth!" it made me exclaim, as though that sentence could logically and completely encompass all the contradictions of the universe. Down in Lahore—so yellow in June, so green in September—enough of the aura stayed with us that we nearly got married, not once, but twice, out of a sheer spirit of comedy.

But the *hodi*-woman, where is she? Learning to understand the geographic spread of Lahore, to take for granted its ravishing asymmetry. She found that as a town it was demanding, collecting frequent tolls on the average traveler's appreciation of perversity. Tiny annoyances—electrical breakdowns, open drains, beggars in the streets like locusts— she had expected, and they did not bother her. What puzzled her was the city's habit of behaving like a mirage, its Cheshire cat ability to disappear. She cited the uncanny approach to Lahore, when the exhausted traveler on the Grand Trunk Road passes Jahāngīr's Tomb on the distant left and hastens across the River Ravi, supple and elegant on the outskirts of the old city. One would have spent much longer taking pleasure in the Ravi, Mustakori claimed, had not Shah Jahān chosen to steal its fire by building the Bādshāhi Mosque so close to the river, adjacent to the old Mughal fort. And on this score Mustakori was actually right: she had located the piercing impact of Lahore. How many times have we driven down from Rawalpindi, fatigue in the marrow of our bones, to cross the full Ravi and then the empty Ravi riverbed, finally to see the great luminous minarets of the mosque rising in our vision like a gasp or a plea? Of course, nothing in the city quite lives up to the promise of such a welcome, so that somehow one is always expecting to find Lahore without quite locating it. I used to find it perverse myself, that aura of anticipation, until it occurred to me that the town has built itself upon the structural disappointment at the heart of pomp and circumstances and since then I have loved to be disappointed by its streets. They wind absentmindedly between centuries, slapping an edifice of crude modernity against a medieval gate, forgetting and remembering beauty, in pockets of merciful respite.

When Mustakori first arrived, she at once fell victim to the vagaries of the city and wanted a vocabulary to do justice to the perfect postcards in her mind. And the word with which she kept rubbing shoulders—dangerously—was "subtlety." "Subtlety": that word cropped up often when

Pakistan attempted to talk about itself in history. It was at the cutting edge of our border with India, that great divide of sibling rivalry: when India described our portion of the map of the subcontinent as ferociously mean and skinny, we bridled and said that actually it was subtle and slim. "Shah Jahān's Taj?" we'd say. "Ah yes," we'd shrug. "His Taj is his Taj, but his Bādshāhi, it is more . . . it is so . . . subtle . . . ," and our sentences would trail to an end, in the nature of exquisite murmurings. Of course the subtlety lingo appealed to Mustakor, who has always responded fulsomely to the possibility of suggestion. During her first year in Lahore, it sent her striding daily up the Mall, past the Punjab University and the High Court, past Kim's Gun and straight into the red museum. (Kipling would have been pleased to see her go, because Mustakori could on occasion pass as Kim trying to pass as a Dravidian.) In the museum, she would seek out the slender Gandhara statue of the fasting Buddha and its lovely intricacies of sinew and rib. There, she would frown at it, trying to locate the subtlety principle, instead only feeling flummoxed by the obviousness of it all. That she should feel flustered staggered me. "Can't you see," I tried to explain, "that you aren't being stupid at all? that Lahore plays on the enchantment of the obvious? that it is arrogant because it refuses to be anything besides what it seems to be?" At this point we were sitting in a tiny roadside cafe at the edge of the Anārkalī bazaar, where Faze was drinking mango milk shake and I was drinking peppered *kanji*. On that morning Mustakor had perfected beyond all normal ken an ability not to see which made her terribly nervous about what a subtle thing the obvious can be. After having tried out every angle of possible explanation, I was finally driven to the dead end of proverbs—"wisdom in the vernacular," as our Urdu tutor used to say—as the only way to alleviate my extreme sense of irritation. It was a relief to turn away from Mustakori's anguished engagement in her mango milk shake and toward the sour calm of idiomatic Urdu. "Is the brain bigger or the buffalo?" my exasperation most quietly asked. "Buffalo!"

blurted Mustakor. Then she ran, and would not stay for a reply.

Something, however, withered the subtlety lingo out of Mustakori's system while she was at Kinnaird, or at least she eliminated it from her diet, as was her wont, just like the time she gave up living on sandwiches made of white bread and potato chips or when she substituted camisoles for sex in the scheme of her creaturely comforts. The latter was the more momentous occasion for us all, the day when we as her friends could look at one another and say, "Dale and Chris, you know what's happened, don't you?" And there would be no question about it, whoever was the respondent: "Yes." "But she's given up sex in the name of . . . ?" I tried out this conversation with ten of Mustakori's friends and was thrilled almost to fear by their unerring response. "Camisoles," they said, "She's taken up with camisoles." Then one would bite his lip, and another gaze around in incredulous dismay.

If anyone came closest to predicting this astonishing feat, it was my sister Ifat, who could think of Mustakor only as Mowgli anyway. They were a funny pair to watch together, with Ifat nearly twice as tall as Mustakori, both of them walking along like ill-assorted French pastries but always able to laugh at jokes invisible to the rest of the company. Once, during National Tree-Planting Week, when the spirit of renovation was rife in the city, Ifat firmly tucked Mustakori under her arm and took her off to rehabilitate her wardrobe. They went to Anārkalī, the old bazaar, and there Ifat tried to tempt Fancy with prints and voiles and *kurtas* of diaphanous white. But Mustakori only turned a dusky blush at each suggestion, shook her head and looked away, until "But why, Mowgli, why?" was all that Ifat had left to say. "Because, mumble mumble," Mustakori meekly replied. Ifat's face lit up at that, as she later told us: "Of course I knew what Mowgli was up to, so I told her that just because she has no breasts at all does not mean that she should be ashamed of such a dandy pair of nipples!" Tillat and I looked askance at that, uncertain how Mustakor would respond to such advice.

But Ifat was now reclining on an afternoon chitchat bed and beginning to enter her finest conversational fettle. She stared off somewhere, picturing Mustakor in pink. Then she talked on in a pleased manner. "I looked at her and said, 'Mowgli, shame on you! how could you malign your nipples in such a way!'" As palm trees were to the Saharan plain, Ifat told her, so Mustakori's lactating-looking nipples were to the endearing concavities of her frame. "Think of Poe, and 'The Purloined Letter'!" Ifat exclaimed, losing me. "I mean that Mowgli doesn't need to cram up her appearance with knickknacks, as though those nipples were somehow purloined from a milking mother," she added, with disgust at my stupidity. "I tried to make her take to camisoles, but though you can lead a horse to water, you cannot saddle a cow." And the three of us nodded at that, quite thoughtfully. Years later, that conversation returned to me when Mustakori showed me her first camisole and all that it implied. But though Ifat as ghost will never admit it, all she knew was that camisoles were in the offing. She did not know that they would succeed sex.

But now I am anticipating the overthrow of a regime that didn't occur until years later, for the petticoat government of Mustakori's camisoles began only in her post-Beijing American sojourn. Her conversation with Ifat, however, had taken place in Lahore shortly after we had graduated from Kinnaird and were left glancing about a bit in order to guess what would happen next. "What next, Mustakor?" I said jauntily, and "What next, Sach?" came her rather wan reply. We were clearing out her room in B-Hostel at the time, and the next thing she did impressed me. She picked up her Coca-Cola bottle nipple and actually threw it away. It had stood in her room next to her mattress for all the years I had known her and was, in fact, the only unusual object in the room. When I first walked into Mustakori's room to have a cigarette, I noticed the nipple with a vague unease; only weeks later, however, when our conversation was in full stream, did I feel familiar enough to ask her why she had a nipple that belonged to a baby's bottle on the floor next to her bed. "For Coke," she replied pragmatically. "I tried putting a nipple on a Coke bottle so that when I lay in bed reading, I didn't have to sit up each time I needed a drink." Not even noticing my astonishment, she added, "It didn't work." I was silenced: I could dimly grapple with the concept of an eighteen-year-old wanting to drink from a nippled bottle, but to give that desire such flabbergasting publicity broke the limits of my imagination. So I was impressed when, at the age of twenty-two, the prospect of a future made Mustakori pick her Coca-Cola bottle nipple and definitively throw it away.

This was during the Bhutto era, of which my father was an angry opponent; he sat at home to write, scrawling off article after article on the decline of Muslim nationhood. His was a more thundering "What next?" than ours, and it tended to drown out less vociferous options. As a result, he did not notice that I had my task urgently delineated for me: "Stave off marriage," said my will, "keep it at bay." When Kinnaird opened its gates to let the marriageable out, I quickly took refuge in Punjab University; Mustakori, not really ready to return to East Africa, decided she might as well follow suit. "What a good girl that Sara is!" people beamed, "How she loves to study!" And daily I escaped from the university to run up the breathless stairs of Ewing Hall, dizzy by the time I had climbed high enough to smile at David. In that order, things were peaceful for a while, except that my father was so busy writing his fiery articles that he forgot to tell me about all the kindly innuendos that his childhood friend, Dr. Sadik, had begun to make about my age and the age of his son—and not just innuendos, either. In Pakistani lingo, clear insinnuendos themselves. Finally my father guiltily and gruffly announced that Dr. Sadik was arriving from Karachi that morning, so I was to stay at home. "Why, Pip?" I asked suspiciously. "Oh," Papa blustered, pretending to be noisily absentminded, "he's in town for some silliness . . . some wedding business . . . ," and I knew at once what would come next. "Whose wedding, Papa?"

"Where is my pen!" he suddenly shrieked, thrashing about the bed as though in water. But I waited so sternly that he could not postpone any longer. "Yours," he lamely said.

And thus I found myself sitting out in the garden, being beamed at by Dr. Sadik. As soon as we were in our chairs, the euphemisms began careening back and forth, and I, wary of the pitfalls in Urdu politesse, felt danger leap up inside me. Sadik smiled his affable smile and said that he had always loved me as though I were his daughter; I told him a trifle sourly that my hands were quite full enough with fatherly love. Slow to affront, he genially performed the next round of his minuet, assuming that my recalcitrance was some pleasure-prolonging device that licensed me to hide my concord up my sleeve for some time more. His son, of course, was not on the scene, and neither were my parents, both of whom ran turncoat, inventing the most improbable excuses. My mother gave a ravishingly absentminded smile and disappeared into Welshness, as though she had stumbled upon some hidden cultural ritual that she was too polite to disturb. My father concocted a journalist's crisis and scuttled off heavily to his study. I could see him from where I sat, writing cross-legged in his worn green armchair, occasionally glancing at the garden guiltily. "What next," I thought bitterly, "will they design to do with me?"

The shadows in the garden grew longer; Dr. Sadik's kind eyes grew more distressed; I dug my nails into the palms of my hands and repeated, no. The weight of my impoliteness sat so heavily upon us that we felt equally aghast, seeing the ritual of centuries being perverted into such threadbare obstinacy. By nightfall I know that both he and I could have fallen onto the humid grass of a Lahore evening and hugged each other into sleep and its obliterated comfort. It set a bond between us to be struggling there, as though on Everest, in our desire to be polite. Indeed, I felt almost pained when Dr. Sadik, with the dignity of a person rejected, gravely left; "Stop, dear man!" I wished to cry, "I am your partner in that dignity!" Within a year Dr. Sadik had found another bride for his son, and he and my father resumed their fifty-year intimacy. On the heavy day that Sadik left our house, however, and I went seeking confrontation with my parents, all I found was Papa gazing philosophically at his cigar. "Sara," he said, "today you have made me lose my oldest friend. But far be it from me to reproach you for it." "Oh, you preposterous person!" I exclaimed and left him, his lion's head reclining amid wreaths of smoke. "What next, Sach?" Mustakori weakly asked that night. "Reality principle time," I grimly answered. So the next morning we both got up and joined the Caravan Theater.

The year of Caravan Theater was a sunny time, taking our somewhat motley company to different cities, setting up stage in Karachi and Peshawar and Lahore. We made some invaluable additions to our theatrical vocabulary, particularly from pockmarked and swashbuckling Jamil Bismil, also known as the dashing Jimmy B. He was famous in the Lahore Arts Council as being a past master of "cut-to-cut dialogue," which signifies a rapid unpunctuated exchange between two actors. "Speed up the wrath scene, Saira!" I was urged. "Real cut-to-cut, my dear!" And if Jimmy B. taught us how to cut-to-cut, then it was Khan Sahib who gave us the equally important concept of taking laughters. Khan Sahib, elderly and silver-streaked, took a paternalistic pride in the younger talents of the Caravan Theater, lecturing us earnestly about the selfless joys of the stage. Once, during a Peshawar performance, I bumped into him backstage when the success of the evening was making him shiver with glee. "Audience is eating tonight!" Then he punched my shoulder in sheer comradeship. "Did you see how many laughters Jimmy B. took in scene 2? *Yar*, he took five laughters, that Jimmy B.!" And he nodded five times, in significant delight.

By this era, Mustakori had left the stage and had taken up instead with sound and lighting, having become enamored overnight with the array of buttons and levers—those nipple look-alikes—that this new profession had put in front of her, with all the glamour of a keyboard. In our Caravan Theater travels, I was one of the actresses, Perin Cooper was the other, while Mustakori came along as a backstage boy, a hand for all seasons. She would sit in a little glass room at the back of various theaters, changing our light and modulating our sound. Once, in the middle of an O'Neill death scene, I realized that something had been botched, because suddenly I found myself competing with a voice that should not have been there. It was Mustakor's. She had muddled her microphones, and instead of talking to someone backstage, she was filling the auditorium with a sibilant whisper: "Perin," Mustakori hissed, "tell Sara to do her buttons up!" I froze. Khan Sahib, trying to die, looked pained. But our audience was enchanted, taking up with cut-to-cut gusto the refrain, "Sara, do your buttons up! Sara, do your buttons up!" Buttoning this particular dress had always been an annoyance to me, since its pleats and folds invariably opened into rows of tight-waisted hooks and eyes. Which buttons, I mused, envisioning flesh. Then, in an extraordinarily deft move, Jamil Bismil walked catlike onto the stage in defiance of O'Neill's intentions: he threw a shawl about me, smiled, and left. The hall fell silent, and Khan Sahib proceeded to die, with considerable relief in his voice. That night, at curtain call, Jimmy B. took more than five laughters from our audience, for he had given them the finest play of all when he strode on in my defense like a playboy of the eastern world.

Playing that death scene in the Caravan Theater year, however, vexed me secretly, because it made me feel disloyal to the spectacle I had witnessed three years ago, in the winter of the 1971 war. It was the day of the cease-fire, and trying times had just begun: Mustakor had flown back to the safety of Kenya, while Ifat and I were living with her father-in-law in Rawalpindi, none of us knowing the fate of Javed Mawaz, the brigadier's son and Ifat's husband. What strange news came into the house that day, miseries almost incapable of believing in their own reality! One poignancy I learned was that the younger brother of my old friend T.K. had been killed an hour before cease-fire in the tank battle at the Sargodha border. By the time I reached their house, the funeral had begun. T.K.'s brother's body had been packed by the army into a wooden crate, which sat on the driveway of the family home, surrounded by keening village mourners, until T.K.'s mother emerged and pushed them away. A stern woman, with Pubjabi cheekbones and deep-set eyes, she went to put her arms around the box that held her son. A splinter snagged the palm of her hand: she looked at it and frowned. Then she turned to the crowd and asked, "Why did they put this box around my son? Couldn't they have made it look like a coffin?" All of us, in a communal moment of hideous imagining, suddenly realized the pieces that the box contained, and moved to hold the mother back as she maddened herself with monotony. "Open the box, open the box," she wailed. Three years later, I distressed myself by playing an O'Neill death scene in unconscious imitation of Tarik's mother. I liked the scene, knowing that my expression felt familiar, but it made me wince when I remembered, "Oh, so there's where I found that gesture, that inflection." I wished to give that spectacle better respect than to bandy it about in the cause of entertainment, but nothing could break the habit: I was T.K.'s mother for every night of Caravan Theater's version of O'Neill. The funeral itself was such a medley swirl that T.K. and I did not exchange a word until it was time to leave: "Oh my dear, my dear," was all I could find to breathe.

Mustakori did not see my drift when I told her of my misgiving, trying to explain that I did not want to be a plagiarist of my own experience. She just looked puzzled. "But isn't acting always drawn from life?" she asked with the air of someone aiming at enlightenment. "Go find yourself a camisole," I responded in disgust. In those days—directly after Caravan Theater—Mustakori lived in the metaphor of clothing, so she had no objection when my language lingered among the lingerie, to borrow her own ill-turned phrase. For when theater ended and I returned to Punjab

University, Faze did too, except that she also turned to advertising, henceforth walking like a slogan hunter through the world. Her natural genius for the profession was astonishing. "What a bold-faced hussy your psyche must really be," I marveled, "to let you think of Cook Me Quick." I would grudgingly allow for the Such Stuff as Dreams mattress, but the Cook Me Quick packet of dried curry sauce struck me as nothing other than obscene. The advertising company, however, adored her way with words and hailed as a total success her campaign for Fabron, the Great Getaway in Fashion Fabrics. Often did we—whistling in embarrassment—change the subject while driving with Mustakori over the Zafar Ali Road Bridge in Lahore when she insisted on gazing with pride at the neon-lit Fabron advertisement saying, "That slogan's mine!" "Watch that fabric," Mustakori's slogan flashed, "under stress and under strain . . . " The strain was too much for us, so we'd look away.

It was the Fabron campaign that gave Fancy Musgrave her new name, Faze Mackaw. She began to dress like a cockatoo in all kinds of unlikely colors, yellow trousers, shirts of red and blue. "That Tanzanian transvestite," said Shahid distinctly, "wears the clothes of a macaw." He was home from Cambridge for a summer in Lahore. "I mean the bird!" he added irritably. "I do not know the clan!" And immediately it took, the Mackaw appellation. Loving Shahid as I did, I was pleased to have him home, sleeping on a rooftop adjacent to my room, where I could amble over for a good-night chat. One evening, sitting on the edge of his sweet-smelling *nivar* rope bed, I was startled to find a tiny yellow feather lying inadvertently beneath his shoulder: it made me smile at Shahid, kiss his neck, and then leave him to whatever his great hooded eyes allowed him to conceive. That summer, dressed in Fabron red and green, Faze Mackaw changed names like clothes, getting up as Fancy and going to sleep as the Fonz. It rapidly became our favorite game, to see the permutations we could put to Mustakori's name, tossing it around like a beach ball on sultry afternoons. "Where's

63

Fuschia?" Ifat would shriek with a gleam of maniacal inventiveness. "Where's Fuschia McKey?" "And where is Footsie Moose?" Tillat replied. Shahid won the palm, though, on the day when Mustakori discovered her connection with Zaire and spent half an hour describing Belgian colonial practice in Africa as a preamble to the announcement that her dad the judge had eaten supper with Mobutu the previous week. The story finally over, Shahid looked up in pain: "A most succinct rendition, Congo Lise."

I did not see Shahid for four years after that August, the last time all of us congregated under a single roof. By the next time we met, Mamma was already in her grave and the famine had begun. Still, we managed to have a merry enough time one summer, Shahid and Faze Mackaw and I. We spent the weekends driving around the English countryside looking for picturesque pubs, a relatively easy goal, or we lay on the grass watching cricket, bemused by the ball's hypnotic plock in the lasting light of summer nights. But something of the set had been broken, and I never knew when I would look up to notice, like a miracle, Shahid's eyes fill up with tears. It made him angry at me, and he brushed off my consolation as though it were a fly or an errant bee. "I love you for the owl you are," he made me think, "and all the ways you choose to glare at me."

During the drought that began in 1978, in the blistering year that my mother died, Mustakori initiated a long process of unlearning how to sit in the presence of my siblings and me. In the beginning, when Faze and I would meet in the American Midwest, I could not quite understand the new nervousness of her manner or the things that made her flag and drag even in ordinary traffic. It was as though her early twenties had invited her to complete a task of urgent forgetfulness, and her decorum had no choice but to go through the gestures of a long dismantling. Then I began to realize that Fancy Musgrave could no longer look at my face without vividly imagining its possible demise, so it was easier for her not to look at all, fond as she was of me and of my siblings. By an unfortunate accident, she was in my kitchen building a bookshelf on the morning in March when Western Union called to tell me that Ifat had been killed. Poor Mustakor. She watched my face scream and in some pristine way has never looked at me again, despite all the post-Ifat hours we have spent together. First I screamed, then I sat down at a kitchen table—Dale's oak square—and tried to concentrate my mind on what should happen next. Fully convinced of her own inability to comfort, Mustakori crept into the bathroom and then came to set in front of me a box of tissues for my tears, poor palliatives. And so I said, to cheer up my grief, "It must be the Kleenex Company, Faze." As the wan joke was uttered, I learned two things. I saw, appalled, that my will was already convalescent, crawling back to life. And, through the blind panic that crossed Mustakori's face, I could anticipate: "This girl will never want to look at me again."

She hasn't. Many long hours, of course, we have since spent together, walking city streets in comrade blues, but that's a different matter. In the months following Ifat's funeral a brittle gaiety became my wont, as though I had folded up my aura and put it in my pocket, so little did I want to be seen of me. One day Mustakor came walking over from the mews (her flat was known as the mews, mine as the mansion) to say with finality, "Sach," in the manner of one who reads revelation into names. "What next, Zorro?" I asked. "I want a rest from the West," she replied, with a spark of her former Fabron-girl flair. "I'm leaving America and going to China." "You are?" I raised my eyebrows at her skinny monkey expression, although there was a hilarity to her plan that quite appealed to me. "I'm going to teach at the Beijing Teacher's College, and in the summer holidays I'll go over to Hong Kong and see if I can look up my great-uncle Wong." I had to admit, it was a dandy plan. So Mustakori packed her bags and would not look at me or anyone on the day that she left, flying due west into a perpetual dawn. "What you would love most," she wrote to me some months later, "are the rooftops. They have a slant that would ravish you." For, as an oblique reparation for her inability to look at me again, Mustakor had slipped into the habit of looking at the world as if through my eyes. It made me worried, to think of her bungling up my rods and cones, so I insisted that she put my vision back where it belonged.

For two-odd years Mustakori lived in the Friendship Hotel, home of foreign experts in Beijing, and she churned out letters like a hurdy-gurdy trundle machine. They all had winsome stamps, the letters and packages that wended their way in my direction, coming as colorful touches of exotica to where I was now living, amid the small Berkshire Hills. When we read her letters, I and recipients like Dale or Chris, we felt amazed at how much Fancy's new life seemed to leave her untainted by experience, as though her wisdom consisted in remaining pure of any knowledge that travel pretended to confer. Chinese joined the company of Urdu and Swahili and French, languages with which Mustakori had once shaken hands but with which she somehow never developed an intimate relationship. Yet she drove a bicycle daily through the city, claiming that cycling is the only private activity available to the townsfolk of Beijing, and learned to eat deep-fried pork fat in Dining Hall No. 1. If not her vocabulary, then at least her expertise trebled, for she suddenly began teaching courses in Freud and Christianity and Western civilization with a primitive energy that took even me by surprise. I was teaching too, some thousands of miles away, but only in an abstracted fashion: that was the autumn when the world turned empirical for me, and while Mustakori's post–Cultural Revolution students devoured Dora and the Wolf-Man, I taught myself how to love Richard X as intently as I could.

Visiting him up in smoke-smelling skunk-land was like the heart of darkness in my book, a piece of outer space. He would cook for me beneath his huge barn roofs, and one evening interrupted himself to say, rueful and accusatory, "You'll say about me, 'He used to cook for me.'" "Yes," I answered judiciously, "I probably will." For I liked to watch his frugal gestures as he cut and pared, his fingers conscious of my watching him. At that point I had not fully learned the trick of his mind, his habit of anticipating the past tense in every story, so now I realize that he must have thought of me as completely lost to him, even before he had quite finished laying eyes on me. It gave him a slight frown sometimes, a shadow, as though I seemed as illusory to him as the ambiance of Lahore. When I noticed his face take on that cast, I felt impelled to interrupt, to insist on some idiot truth: "I'm nice. I'm real." But the closest I could get would be to say, "What are you thinking?" and then we would gravely chat about some sundries, punctilious as betrayal.

Grave autumn colors to those days. Ifat still felt unburied—to me she still was warm—and, somewhere south, Richard's mother lay dying, causing him tight-lipped pain. It could end tomorrow or drag on for years, he said, which is why she could not come to stay with him for good. "Why not?" I asked. We were driving through the hills, as was our wont, and I was smoking cigarettes. "Because it would ruin my life," he flatly said. I admired him, then, for facing that gray guilt and the twist of pain that it set throbbing in his temple, though I knew it was easier to be invaded by a body than by a notion, and Richard bore the notion of his mother perpetually around him, like a plea. It made me grip his thin thigh in pity for us both, thinking, "Don't you see? She already has moved in, sweetheart; she will be with you for your life." For something about Richard allowed me to think in simples, and I felt grateful for that little piece of liberty amid the various tyrannies of our routine.

Long before Mustakori returned to take up again the saga of her unfinished degree, I had mislaid Richard—or he me, since it is now hard for me to determine who was the cause and who the effect of that somewhat sorrowful parting. That he was with me, and then was not, is the only simple way of putting things. There was a voice that used to say to me, "Put back your body where your life belongs," but I have never been particularly good at heeding that piece of advice, happy instead to let life and body go grazing off to their own sweet pastures. By now I think they would be petrified with shyness ever to wake up and find themselves bedmates: one makes the bed, the other lies in it, and so are our household duties apportioned. Used to that little schizoid trick, Mustakor was content to know Richard X only as a narrative device in my letters or a figure of speech for my all-time favorite subjects, like loving or understanding things.

When Mustakori came back—a little more wizened, with a shock of gray hair, but fundamentally the Mowgli of yore—we took some time off with Dale and Chris to chat a while, catching up with our now disparate lives. As we sat together in a reuniting coven at Café Chinezipur, Mustakori began to hold forth with great gusto; I looked at her with affection, thinking what a nice voice she had, how funny and familiar! As she talked on, the voice grew more and more familiar, giving me the strangest sense of déjà vu, but it was only when Fancy darted a guilty glance in my direction that I finally realized what she had done. She had pilfered my voice! In my absence, ventriloquized me to a T! I was the man making foolish faces; while she was the chatterbox on my knee! I was astonished, feeling like an organ-grinder who had woken up to discover that the monkey had run off with his machine. "Mustakori," I said very firmly, "give it back to me." For a second, she looked as though she considered feigning ignorance. But then, "I'm glad I had you for a while," she said most cheekily.

Having taken the conversational wind out of Mustakori's sails, I was relieved to note that at least her manner still remained her own. She slumped at the table, lying low over her plate, and constructed perfect forkfuls of food: these thrust into her mouth, she was ready to nod herself back into the conversation, her cheeks jolly with rapidly oscillating cannonballs. Sustained, she begged us to let her undo her corded bales and show us just something of the merchandise she had brought with her from China. Then she gave us all our gifts—a Chinese name for each of us, carved onto an ivory chop and accompanied with a wad of reddest ink— after which she suddenly began behaving as though she were on stage again, opening her wooden trunk with a mysterious air, like Perin Cooper's Prospero of fifteen years earlier. The lid agape, a hundred colors met our eyes, and we fell back dazzled by her array of camisoles. There were a hundred of them, she told us, tailored to her intent design, like a flock of hummingbirds! a shoal of tiny colored fish! a grove of orna-mental peppers! "I've returned," said Mustakor to me, in a half-tearful and half-bashful chuckle, "with a prodigal coat of many colors." And then, "I'll break my staff, and deeper than did ever plummet sound, I'll drown my book." So Mus-takori murmured. But when she looked around, the stage was nowhere to be found.

Fancy M. actually finished her degree in the year that followed, and got a teaching job in a nearby metropolis. Mustakori would still come to visit me, of course, in order to wash clothes, but with the hesitance of a latecomer, ab-stracted into tardiness. Occasionally we would take a daylong holiday together, which essentially meant that we would start walking through city streets early in the morning and still be walking late at night. Stepping soberly one day, in an apple-eating frame of mind, I attempted to assess my last ten-year American span. "Has it been a Decade of Development?" Mustakori—quoting General Ayub—cautiously essayed, her glance in my direction falling a second short of my face. "Well, I've never been at a loss for schemes, but it's been a little hard to keep them tidy, all those Five-Year Plans": this I admitted as we stared out at a soupy city ocean on a tired dock. "I must say, I've had to devalue my currency a couple of more times than I liked," I added, following a sea gull's strut. After a while, "So have I," Mustakori confessed. Our conversation brought crabbing to mind, crabbing at night in the Karachi harbor during Caravan Theater's off-hours. We dangled quiet thoughts into the water until our sentences happened to tug us, once in a while, into the kind of startlement that says: "My goodness—there's actually a crab at the end of my line!"

"Why weren't you better at it?" By the time Mustakori blurted out this question, my mind had been an hour in Pakistan. "At what?" "Oh, conservation, saving things," she wailed, uncertain of her boldness in chiding me. I answered in the only way I could: "Think of it this way—I'm dandy at expenditure." Mustakor half-looked at me and then let her foreshortened gaze slide back into the water. It struck me as a bonus, then, to be given a veil for thirty-three summers' worth of face fatigue. "Why weren't we among those who build!" she suddenly exclaimed, rippling like a pebble into water. "Try not to be too stupid, Chatterbox," I reproached. ("Tom dropped by, Sach," Mustakori had said nervously, "and we had a wee wee chat"—this, when I was engrossed in mourning for that tall imbecile; on the spot we dubbed her "Wee-Wee Chatterbox, Jr.") "I can easily see you as a Baskin-Robbins girl, building all sorts of fancy shapes." That cheered her up. "And I can see you," Mustakori added with inspiration, "as supervisor of the daytime shift in an affection factory. I can just see you bullying them into shape, scores of affection-pacemaker machines." We arose then, to amble on some more, heartened by the wholesomeness of talk.

"Listen," I said, as we went sauntering, "I'll tell you what I think." Ignoring her habit of nodding before I had said a word, I went on, "I have been, Mustakori, the Dutch to your Amsterdam." "The Dutch?" She looked blank. "I mean the psyche repair work I've done for you," I explained irritably, "the way I've reclaimed your mind from swampy nothing into land." And I was right; when I first met Mustakor, a heron would have declined to land on such a quivering surface. "Why, they could build an airport on you now!" And Fancy must have got my point, for after a while she said, "And I have been, Suleri, Hans Brinker to your dike, "—quickly adding, as I bridled, "I mean your friends do tend to get pushed up against it, your will to go crashing into liqui-

70

dity." And then she looked a little nervous and self-congratulatory at having arrived at such a formulation. I told her in a kindly way that she was stealing my voice again but that somehow where I sounded merely figurative, she managed to be obscene. "No, no!" protested Mustakori, "I know you to be a very modest woman, chaste in the extreme." That pleased me. "Thank you, Mustakor. And you're the same yourself." "Thank you, Sach," she solemnly said.

Mustakori's final continental shift, her American return, seems to have slowed her pace down slightly: she no longer anticipates quite so blithely the next installment of what may possibly come next. Perhaps it is the wear of work, but we've noticed that, if not actually roots, then she has certainly begun to dangle filaments from her elbows and her wrists, like a gnarled but baby banyan tree. And if she has not been able to visit Meru for a while, then the mountain periodically comes to Muhammad, bringing the clan of the Mustakoris to her door. Great families of cousins suddenly arrive—Andy, Pandy, Hoola, Hoopa, Rusti, Brusti, and Tim—drenching the streets with Mustakori look-alikes, the kitchen sunlight band. After the last invasion, a touch of the old Fabron twitch returned to Fancy: "Go find yourself a legend, then return," she quoted from some forgotten rhyme. Then she sighed, as one burdened sighs. It made me look more curiously at her face and how it hid behind its plea, its smallness. "If you want unknown territory, there's always intellection— you can find virgin soil within you, happier by far," I said in a sprightly manner, rallying round. But in her middle age Mustakori prefers to be monkey to her own moods alone, like one of those wizened little Lahori performance apes, dancing to the tune of a different monkey-man's drum. *Dug-Duggis*, those miniature drums are called.

So that's my story of perfect ignorance. The proof of the pudding is that Mustakori's dimpleless dough remains uncooked, to be relished only by some future imagination. But we must be careful. Having migrated at the half-decade for most of her life, it would be part of her perfect perversity to attempt to transmigrate, too, and that's an eventuality we must decidedly quash. For as Tillat declares, "The thought of having to cope with such a skinny-mooded ghost gives me the heebie-jeebie creeps!" In my time, too, I have had disturbing glimmerings. Consider the month I went back to spend the first post-Ifat June at home in Lahore, frozen, on my bed, unable even to sweat. How oddly I thought of Mustakor when her birthday gift to me that year read, in the garbled white-on-pink of homely Pakistani cables, "HAMLET COME HOME WRITE YOUR BOOK IT WASTES THE YEARS YOU WANDER STOP LOVE HORATIO STOP."

# GOODBYE TO THE
# GREATNESS OF TOM

He made things: that I think was it, in the early days of my lack of custom with such prodigious tangibility. When I first noticed that great spate—those pictures and bookish oddments, all sorts of stuffs diversely dyed—my own merely indifferent talent for construction knew it had no choice but to lend complete support, on an installment plan, to a man of such efficient invention. By that year too I think I had not yet had my fill of educating America, as though it were my bounden duty to talk a borderline around each encounter that came my way in order to contain it in a peculiarly private grammar. Tom of course was big, but even aside from him, what trouble my conjugations caused me! They sent me opening doors and breaking bottles in each established decorum that I would most have liked to have examined intact, but then I had still to conceive of America as a place that bespoke its own establishment. So Tom's large head seemed a miraculously obvious place to begin: even today, that great expanse of face makes my own folly seem proportionally paltry in relation to the unswerving truths of size.

Coming from Pakistan, I think I was still colored by the sense that I officially belonged to a populace that could not afford to think of size. It was simply too deranging, for none of us really liked to contemplate the fact of our own numbers, in themselves quite sizeable, and how we now clung with precarious novelty to our designated swoop of the globe. We picked up that segment and quickly colored it green, but not all the leafy vegetables of the world could obscure our knowledge that independence—a big word—actually signified a slivering up of space. When in 1947 Mountbatten's scissors clipped at the map of India and handed over what Jinnah fastidiously called a moth-eaten Pakistan (we had been unrealistically hungry for the whole of the north—and Delhi, too, I think), the more energetic Muslims of the subcontinent winced to see that they could push and push at their cuticles, only to discover meager half-moons. But those very people must have worked with speedy fidelity all through the crazy winter of 1946, realigning their spatial perspective with something of the maniacal neatness of a Mughal miniaturist. Evidently, they were prepared to put behind them the geography of perpetual dismantling that appears to suggest, for Indians, pragmatic life. Instead, that shrugging motion had been suddenly petrified, until there was no more Benares to shun and no Delhi in which to sew silently the shroud of courtly Urdu. I was born after all of this, so it is not truly the excuse I can use, not being the business of my generation. But I often wonder at them, those brand-new Pakistanis, being walked into the world as though into a hotel room—or a concept as tidy and as brittle and intact. They tell me nightmare trains had wailed them there, clattering irreversibility over the tracks of that long unmaking. They arrived unkempt, but pleased. It was what they had asked for, after all.

Close on four decades later, size is still not exactly in currency, not in the Punjab, nor in Sind, nor in any of the five—no, four, lacking Bangladesh—provinces of Pakistan. Balance, I'd say, is the word we want, its euphemism tautly strung like all the crazily overloaded telephone wires that scribble ill-connection from center to urban center. The land between is perforce lost in such postures of concentration, but what price earth when tiny bones of disequilibrium keep chattering about once-and-future partitions in your head? Even the plough in that still largely agricultural land moves to divide stiff spine of soil from spine in the consciousness that what one wins, the other loses. It makes for a people who, however hungry for ownership, seem more at home with signing deeds on paper than with the ground on which they stand. When I think of space, I'm quite like that. In geography my wherewithal can flag. It is rarely able to lay hands on the shape of a city, or intuit north from south in any given continent, its up from its down. In the Lahore of my girlhood I had a friend called Ayla, who achieved moments of uncanny serenity by combing the city for pockets of unfamiliarity: once found, she would look at them with relief and say, "I'm lost." That game never required much exertion on my part, except that I was always curious to see how the monuments of greater- and lesser-known Lahore should for the asking so step out of context, hold the gesture, and then disappear.

It was like trying to locate what possessed Tom's cycle. For to cast him into landmass from the start is to overlook how we first hit upon acquaintance. Just as completely as Ferozepur Road could turn upon its steady bend and poise for a moment in space, so it makes me shiver slightly to recall that yes, in Tom's story, a cycle is where it all began. I refer to no comforting Vespa, the likes of which my poor relative Bashir went chugging on through Mayo Gardens, but a vehicle of proportions somewhat military, on whose hindquarters I could only clamber gingerly, and from the left, as though it were a horse. During a quiet summer of northeastern green I learned to incline my shoulders this way and then that, accommodating myself as I had never done before to the shape of a curve or a hill. Tom dropped me from his motorcycle once, leaving shadows of gravel in my skin that—if I cared to—I still could find today. He was most remorseful, but in those days I could not mind, held as I was in a posture of bright askance, rising like a poppy from the fields of my recent dead.

But to travel back thus far is too enfeebling, too bone-wearying a business for my imagination. It is similar to my new reluctance to visit old Muslim tombs and contemplate again what I know I'll find, that inlay of marble on the walls with their curious flat-faced flowers, so dainty and scornful of their own decoration. And then the dead center of the grave can sit so heavily sometimes, surrounded as it is with tiny writing, words like capillaries to tighten in the head, as you read round and round with them all ninety-nine of Allah's appellations. O light, O clarity, O radiance, you read, until suddenly sequence becomes a vertiginous thing, and your brain is momentarily short of blood and breath. I used to enjoy the spaciousness of those places, the shoes-off of it, which put coolness at my feet. Now, I am not sure I would stop to consult those images, even by accident, in a passing book. So Tom's story can never begin back yonder, in his neck of the woods: it has to be here, with travel-ache already over, when I have washed my hands of sequence and can glance at its swarming tiny autonomies in order to hiss, "*Down, wantons, down.*"

Thus error, since error is joy's alternative idiom, must be the geography to involve me in its wry location. With dear Tom my crucial fault was a blurring of vision that allowed me to equate flesh with information, my poison with another's meat. How could I imagine that someone who consumed so much of the great realities of airspace would be chary of acknowledging the technologies of simple articulation, that which keeps distinct and democratic tarsal from metatarsal, rib from cage? What I did not realize at first was that information for him was like a droplet of immense significance, an object visible only through the weight of its capacity to vanish and consequently become a dangerous, guarded thing. "I have known you for five years," I once cried out, "and I don't even know your blood type." All at once my register of poignancy felt wrenched by the pathos of blood types, wracking me with the sheer justice of my claim. Tom was stricken, desperate, and appalled, as streams of information went coursing down my face.

At that point my body must have been craving simplicity—which can never be called Tom's fault. For how can I blame him for those quick shifts of need that kept my genes in marching order, deploying me from front to front? "Badedas—the bath stuff—is boring, Sara," Tillat said to me gloomily in Kuwait one day, "I hate the thought of that green." I could not help but agree that it was trying, to be held responsible for the odors of one's former tastes, as though the sloughing off of cells was not in itself a daily declaration of relief, a little hymn that sang thank god, thank god, I am a two-faced thing. Once, driving back from Kinnaird College to Zafar Ali Road by taxi in truant twilight hours, what a shock I got when my taxi driver pulled over to the side of the road and said, "Sister, let's open our fast." Many lurid images had skeltered through my head before I recollected—the taste of my last cigarette still acrid on my tongue—of course, it is Ramzan, and now the man must eat in order to feel faithful. He gravely handed me a bunch of grapes and then retired to a nearby grassy knoll to put, as Muslims will, heads down and bottoms up in a westerly direction. The meter ticked on, and of a sudden I felt ravished by a grace to which I had no real belonging but whose arrival made me intensely shy. And so I bent my head and ate those pallid grapes, as though I absolutely knew why people should be grateful when made hungry by the course of God.

Thus, long ago, before the past of this particular tale can be said to have officially opened, I had made my peace with the way in which Tom's largess was directly defined against the particularity of information, caught up instead in the logic of its own invention. For I had never met such an invented man. I used to speculate about whether or not his name was the root cause of it, of how deranging it must have been when at twelve that body began growing—and would not stop growing—to have the coverage of only such a fore-shortened name as Tom. Hardly sufficient to clothe the comedy of toes, you'd think, let alone everything else that stood upon them. I could never think of his name without smiling, knowing that it would hardly require the kind of deflation that my sisters and I gave to my father when we looked at his wedge-shaped lion's head and called him Pip or Little P. My siblings of course have long-since eliminated the word "Tom" from their diets, asking instead simply to hear me groan, "How's *Lambu*, Sara, how's *Lambu*—the tall one—now?" So Richard X was *Kutha-wallah*, the dog one; Jamie was always Jamie; and Pea-head Ross had no name at all. But now I have unwittingly opened the vista of a decade that must be packed away: I am too weak to be tourist, and the mess of it pains me, to have someone else's scenes from Seville spilling their concertina over my lap, hurting my eyes with the backside and the front of each connected image. There is too much autonomy to names: let one in and a host of them are bound to follow, dancing round your room in evil capers and cornering your attention where it does not wish to stay.

So it soothes me to recollect how easy it was for Nuz to call Lazarus her cook Nazareth and not notice her mistake even though they lived in the same Karachi house for a substantial period of time. There was only one two-year span, I think, when Tom and I actually lived in the same city and vagabonded together in any routine way. During that era he was building a building, and the bricks and mortar of it all absorbed us both, since I was charmed by the notion that there was any correlation between those airy black-and-white drawings and the structures that they promised to raise. In the careless way that can overtake intimates, we used that building as a unit of time, an ordering principle whose com-pletion would allow us to think of all the different orders that we really ought to construct, as though it could make our decisions for us. Here is where I fault myself, for my lazy trick of deferral that allowed me to believe I could actually locate my own framework in someone else's building. I was too content, I think, with coffee in bed in the morning and a letter at night to bother with even the possibility of flaw in such methods of completion. They were simple schemes of formality, probably conscious of error from the moment of their inception, yet I—caught up in the precisions of how one day suggests another—kept them creaseless anyway. But before I could quite articulate what was happening, the building opened only into more of itself, until what I had assumed was solidity turned out to be its opposite, a structure based on the brittle promise of how much bigger it was still to become. I dreamed once that the building had actually sprouted wings, bronze and heavy mockeries, which strained and heaved against the now obsolete need for steady location. It made my mind blank when I woke up—but how could I do it, become Lilliput to the Gulliver of Tom, when my fingers lacked the staying power of such industry? Instead, I slowly knew myself to be incapable of keeping up with such acts of replication and early began to conceive of Tom as that which must be renounced, forgone. Of course that tripled his value in my head, lending him something of the sharp intake of breath that betokens the conclusions of a cigarette, making of him a mourning-place, monument before his time.

I always have mourned in museums. They remind me too much of how each time you walk into your own room you are forced to take stock of it, to look around and say, "So this is it, my life." When I am taken to a museum—I'd rarely go of my own volition—I am too touched by its exposure to be softened by its equal quietude. I cannot help but wonder why such precise expressions of presentation are so hungry with the desire to please or the will to evoke a self-repeating admiration that will keep the spectator upright from one room to the next. Consequently, instead of following object to object, I am moved to pat something inconsequential like a wall and murmur, "There, there; you have put together money and beauty, complicated things. You have made them seamlessly pretty and that's a job well done, so please relax now; I am satisfied." But then the sheer climate-control of it all will set me sweating, anxious for the sweeter peace of inadvertency and a world less heavy with the expectation of its ability to gratify. If I must mimic the postures of the devout, I think I would rather go to a mosque for the odd half-hour and cool my head in its geometry of complete disinterest, which warns me that I had better soon be gone, before the courtyard is white with men and fallen angels.

I used to think that it would be refreshing to live in a house that was shaped like a mosque, basing its center on empty space, with a long kitchen where the imam should pray and four turret bedrooms, one for every minaret. But Papa cured me of such sentimental schemes. "Take me to a *masjid*," he hugely groaned in the days of my mother's death, "just let me live like a holy man." Now this was preposterous, even for Papa, and tried the patience of his otherwise good-humored children. After a morning filled with sundry references to mosques, "Let's do it," said Ifat, rising with exasperation, "let's unleash him on one." We didn't, but for years later we used the phrase "it's the old *masjid* syndrome," to characterize his, and our own, excesses of self-sorrow. But he did successfully muddy the simplicity of a mosque for me; now I can never walk into one without half-wondering whether that little mumbling man in the corner there will leap up, shout "Surprise!" and turn out to be Pip. It was part of my annoyance the one time I visited the Jamia Masjid in Dehli, one of those Shāh Jahān inventions. After the Bādshāhi of Lahore—a perfect mosque, sitting at an angle to the Ravi River—I was not prepared to take to the bold stripes that marked the Jamia's domes, its angles. But when I reached it, after a hysteric and spindly cycle-rickshaw drive from the Red Fort, the man at the gate would not let me go in. Muslim women were not allowed in the mosque between the hours of *maghrib* and *isha*, he told me, so "of course I'm not a Muslim," I replied. "Then I'll never let you in," he told me smugly, "because I'm the vice-imam." "Then of course I'm a Muslim!" I screamed back. "My grandfather was a Hajji, and my father is a Hajji—he's probably in there now!" It worked as a threat on him as well as it would have on me, and I strode in, undeterred.

There was a time when Tom and I would talk constantly of going to such parts together, so that I could see his version of India, a traveler's vision, and he my more abiding sense of Pakistan. We probably should have visited Lahore at least, so that finally my points of reference could become as physically tangible as himself; but somehow in the daily business of events it became another impossibility, easy to defer. And then I had to realize that such a trip would not be necessary, for we had lost the art of location, and at that point wherever we met East and West had no relevance to the singleness of our exchange. How those conversations and their manner of amazing question withered me, embattling as they did his forms of information against mine, turning all nourishment to straw upon my palate! Oh he still made things, but I had lost my spirit, since his impulse to make had become bigger than ever and acquired a phantasmagoric edge that robbed me of the pleasure I'd taken in the structure of invention. It put him in the air mostly, and when I was not his adversary, he was pitting his will against the dateline, until I feared he would never be able to break the habit of solitary buoyancy. "I am flying to London, Sara," Tom would say, "and then to Germany." I could only be silent. As a sop to the angle of my expression he would quickly add, "And when I'm back, we'll talk." I felt as though I were being offered the consolation that flight attendants present when, one in each aisle, they jointly hold out yellow life jackets. Look how cunningly, they say, each has been equipped with a little whistle and a torch, so that you may call and flash for help, and here's the nozzle you may blow upon in case your catastrophe does not automatically self-inflate! I thought how good it was to know that when I went tumbling through the immensity of that ocean, I could always blow and blow myself to some safe shore.

Thus we became separate working things, spending more time in the hullabaloo of each daylight hour than in the possible serenity of night. I was working too hard, I would tell myself, to have time to think about all the workings of Tom. But secretly I did, more intently than before, to make the notion of him still available to me, a possibility. He must have known some of the same exigencies: once in a while he would still wish to pull me back into the familiarity of his day, calling me with the terrible hesitance of someone who no longer trusts his license to intrude. So he would use, reluctantly, the telephone, ringing me with nothing left to say but, "On Tuesday I'll be in Milan and on Thursday morning in Düsseldorf and then back to Milan" and on and on, straining my geography with so many urbanities that my sense of the plot went totally awry. Some chemicals of tenderness of course would always wake up with a start to the sound of his voice, but listening to that sequence was a terrifying thing, as though I were being methodically slapped by the inevitability of my own irrelevance. Years later I am still surprised to see how something as innocuous as an airline schedule can resound in my head like an echo chamber or the transient memory of tears.

For how can I disallow their occurrence, the brittle dependency of those days? I lived alone but in expectancy, which robbed me of the necessary solace that surely must accrue for those who truly live alone. Still, I was obstinate, determined to assert my enjoyment of the ways of life above all things, thus pleased to cast my eye about the cool spaces of an empty room and murmur, "St. Praxed's ever was the church for peace." And so I waited to conduct the ceremonies of welcome, sitting up a little straighter with the thought that, if not Tom, then tomorrow Mustafa or Dale or Jamie or Tillat would come to visit. It brought to mind that past master poet Mīrzā Ghālib of Delhi and his taut gaiety of phrase that spoke of the age it had been since his lover was his guest, making his home great with conversation that lit candles through the night. I'd think of that when I was visited. But still a stubborn adhesiveness in me made me loath to give up the notion, long after we had done away with the pretence of plausibility, that it was Tom who was the quickening presence of my day. I cannot believe it was as simple as an addiction to the minutiae of losing, although if I said it once, "The theater of my actions is fallen," I said it a hundred times a day. And, all the while, my sense that something had emplotted me gave structure to my days: I could not move, I thought, till I had served my part in someone else's tale.

What an irritant I was to my intimates in those times. "Leave," they would conjure me and then, with angry impatience, "*Leave.*" "Yes," I'd answer with alacrity, "I will!" But barely had the conversation turned its back than I could feel my mind rise up like a supplicant and say, "Give me a habit; let me wear the same clothes from season into season." Or I would wince to admit that my rash claims had failed to acknowledge the precision of things, which left me with nothing worth leaving. And so I never knew quite how I should have responded when Tillat, gazing sorrowfully away from me and out upon the arid stretch of desert-land, said, "Sara, you must learn how to settle now." She was talking about the stringent graces of monogamy. "Oh sister most monogamous," my brain groaned, "how can I tell you what it is to have a hand upon your head that shapes itself unwittingly to someone else's cranium, so that every nerve end of fidelity in you leaps up to exclaim, 'This is not the cup my skull requires'?" I could not tell her, but it weighed upon my visit to Kuwait as one of the several crucial things we did not find space to say, because—before it felt properly ensconced—my time to stay was done. It wrenched me to leave her and her brood: talking creatures all of them, those settlers in the dust.

"What have you got out of this?" said Shahid to me sternly, his manner leaving room only for the most sheepish

83

of response. I replied that I had enjoyed Tom's countenance and the deftness of his hands, so that I was never happier than when sitting in a room while he was doing something and I was doing nothing. And then I praised an hourless sleep, of the kind when limb can lose its contour as limb and a body falls apart with rest's efficacy—I would have gone on, but Shahid could not take such abrasion to his spirit and walked away from my unfinished sentence, silent with indignation and scorn. Left alone, my list could only grow, until for a moment I thought I knew what I wanted: a catalog, that was all. Of course I would entrust its design to no one other than Tom, his knack of matching page to picture, so that I would have something to show Shahid the next time he thus questioned me. For a second it seemed almost plausible that Tom should be punctual for the day he set aside to bring a catalog to me. Already I could see how absorbed I would be by the quality of each reproduction, how much it imaged what it must conceal. He would doubtless talk endlessly about the pragmatics of it all, making me cognizant once more of yet another breed of paper and the amount of midnight oil he surely burned in the cause of its perfection.

But that was years ago. What followed was an era of greater simplicity, my friends and I deciding that we had no further conversation on this score, which by then felt finished, tonally flattened. At about the same time I also stopped writing letters; as inevitably as he had left my day, Tom left my discourse too. It made me move in convalescence for a while: let sleeping giants lie, I would say warily, and widely skirted any subject that might make him stir. He felt like an anachronism of my soul, one that had been assembled in some random way, with all the quaintness of a jury. "It's done, Mustafa," I breathed out, "it's finally done." And, looking at the brighter side of things, "Now I can buy a bigger bed." Mustafa was curious. "Why didn't you before, in all those years?" "Because Tom would have thought I was doing it to make him feel at home, which of course I wanted to, but the notion of my wanting to would have just felt too oppressive." Mustafa glanced up at me, and then away. "Strange girl," she quietly said.

The habit broken, it was sweet relief to me to be spared the follies of each of my stern pronouncements, those bullying little homilies I would deliver up to Tom, litanies of proper behavior that sprang from hidden funds of my corrective zeal. At the time of their uttering I was roundly persuaded by myself, but learned after a while to suspect the lack of conditionality in my own imperative mood. I had gone to school in a convent, that must be it, the fault of a building in which nuns walked in unison to the whirring of a fan. For us their very habit was admonitory, a reminder that our souls were somewhat disheveled, always in flight from the duty instigated by the dawning of each day. But who could think of dawn when already by midday the combination of heat, hunger, and all manner of inkiness sent us wheeling down those quiet corridors impulsively calling for carnival? In those days my friend was that wonderful woman, beautiful Kausar Mahmood, who had artist's hands and whose face always amazed us because it could look like James Mason and Ravi Shankar and Nazrul Islam, the mad Bengali poet, all at the same moment. "Why do photographs always catch me," she once wondered aloud, "before my smile has reached its summit?" Well, she would smile today if she could see my curious transmogrifications and in the cast of my scold or frown recognize continuing traces of Mother Baptist in me.

"How many books have you written?" Mother Baptist said sourly the last time we met in the faded peace of Presentation Convent's parlor. "Not one, Mother," I said in quick self-vindication, and I am almost certain that she grunted with relief. Then we wandered into the interstices of conversation: her vision kept shifting from chair to ottoman, as though attempting to locate what had possessed me to return. By this time she was in her nineties and had long since forgotten what, in relation to Rawalpindi, Ireland could have possibly been. "And did you marry that T.K. lunatic in the airplane?" she suddenly snarled. "No, Mother," I meekly said, and sipped my tea.

Each time I return to Pakistan, I realize that I have quite forgotten what it is, the fragrance of real tea. Long after Tom had become just an aching notion in my head, I went in search of another cure from him, back to the Himalayas of my childhood, the winsome gullies that climb up the hills beyond the more standard attractions of Murree—a mere hill station of a place, with its mall, its restaurants, and its jostle. No, I felt that I hadn't taken in true Himalayan air until we had wound upward over Dunga Gali and up to Nathia, where all at once my sinuses glowed again with a fabulous commingling of wood smoke and green tea. No trying company could stand between me and that exquisite odor: I drank my tea and then went quickly to stand on the sheer verge that separates Pine's Hotel from the greatness of its valley, where my lungs again could breathe as they have never elsewhere breathed.

"Are you better, Sara?" Nuzzi asked me anxiously when I returned to her in Karachi. "I'm best." "Too good!" she exclaimed consolingly. And yet how could I not be well when I was looking at her? The year before, at forty-six, Nuz had lost all her hair; this year she had sprouted a whole head of baby curls as tender as an infant's. "But my dearest," I said after I had held her, "what on earth have you done to your head?" "Don't you know that I was bald?" she squawked. "But hold and behold, it all came back, and it won't stop curling, curling!" So I held and beheld, over the din of Karachi Airport, until we finally decided to wander arm in arm to where Nuz had gaped the car. She had long-since given up parking, having devised instead the method of gaping: she stops her car anywhere she likes, opens hood, trunk, and all four doors, and leaves it sitting there, just gaping by the wayside. "No one will ever tow or touch anything that looks so forlorn," she told me reassuringly. I realized I was out of touch with Pakistan when it worked like a dream.

Living amid the bustling abundance of Nuz, I finally

86

had time to differentiate between my mind's vestigial sense of Tom and what it meant for me to be standing there, out on a Himalayan bluff or next to the southern murkiness of the Karachi sea. They no longer needed to belong to the same terminology now that my idea of him had been consigned to time zones where I was arriving just at the point when he was taking off. It was that Pakistani balance that came to my thoughts, a sharper word than ever now, with Karachi in a state of civil war, the frontier under siege. "The country cannot last," I heard repeatedly, "we have seen this before." So I looked out in the direction of the borderlines and tried to picture their perpetual rewriting, teaching myself to think through and repeat: "Your mind is a metropolis, a legislated thing. The keener your laws the better their breakage, for civilizations will always rise and fall upon your body's steady landscape."

I realized what it meant, when I returned to Miani Sahib. It was my last morning in Lahore, and I wanted to be respectful to the graves of my mother and my sister. Pressed for time, I took a taxi to the Miani Sahib graveyard, sitting as it does just beyond Mozang Chungi, a shrieking moment in one of the several of Lahore's centers. I found the thorn trees and the dust, but once I had passed through Miani Sahib's gates, I was surrounded by a city that I could not read. There were no signposts, and as though desperately late for a dinner, I went on in blundering optimism, certain that each forking path would take me where I belonged. But the hillocks were too similar, and I could not find the ones I wished to find. An hour later the roses I had bought were bruised and limp, perspiring out their shape into my hand: "Alright," I thought, "a grave is what I've been seeking," and laid them down on the probably equally deserving tombstone of one Shorish Kashmiri. I even did a *fateha* for him, and then looked quickly round to be sure I had not been noticed. But even if I had been, what could I have said—"Please take me to the B block of this town, where I am looking for two women who always gave me pleasure when they kept close company?" No, I mused, somewhere amid this thorny ground your bones are still at work, beloved things. Then should I interrupt your private circle of acquaintance to say that I am Sara, living testimony that you most grievously are dead? Stay put where you are; I'll not bother you again by looking for a sealed door that I could bless imperishably, in the way I bless the unreflecting recollection of your love.

My father had a favorite title when he wrote: the name of his third book, the phrase cropped up repeatedly in his articles over the years, the Men and Matters series, as it was tellingly called. So after *Whither Pakistan?*, the book, we also had "Whither Democracy?" and "Whither Martial Law?" and I am almost certain we had a "Whither?" for every trauma that marked our first thirty years. The tone of Papa's voice, however, never lent itself to question marks: the impetus of his questions invariably end up assuming the posture of a threat. I know he is innocent of this tricky locution; he probably never realized how much—in their respective ways—the family and the government quaked when Pip decided it was high time to reproduce, again, his withering rhetoric. "I'll tell you what it is, Shahid," I said slowly to him one evening, sitting on the floor by his London fire on my way back from Pakistan, still watchful for his jibes, "I think that I can write it now." "What? Your academic stuff?" he asked with blunt disinterest. "No!" I exclaimed and tried to reassemble once again my threadbare patience. "I could do a *Whither Pip?* and I could do *Whither Tom?* and *Whither You and Me?* and the whole sorry lot of us if I wished it. I could do it now!" And then a sudden softness crossed his face: he threw back his head, and smiled. "Do it, if you wish it," he most gently said.

So, once, several years ago, I sat upon a hill in another era: it was either Dover or Williamstown; I can't remember now. Beside me, Tom's bald head was like a boulder that had seen recent rain. He sweated, even in the stringency of that light wind, and his eyes glazed, they paled, staring ahead at their own immensity of effort. For Tom was trying to talk to me. Oh yes, I was invested in that conversation, but how much more bound I felt, in necessary compassion, to the gesture of concentration at my side! "So, what shall we do?" I asked judiciously, "since we cannot do what we are doing now?" "No," he said, as though this were fit response, "we cannot do what we are doing now." Then the wind dropped, or something happened: it distracted us for a moment, put fresh air in Tom's sails—he asked me, as he had done on a hundred equivalent occasions, whether I had noticed how in the West one never could be far away, even in the country, from the whir of some machine. Yes, I had noticed, I said gravely. "So what shall we do now?" I repeated, seconds later. "I'll tell you exactly what I feel, Sara, exactly it"—this he said rapidly, a half-sob in his throat. Then he gathered all his strength into one body and faced his old familiar demon, information, regarding him with scorn. "I do not know what we will do," he said to it rather than to me, "but I . . . preclude . . . nothing . . . " And that was it, as far as the concretion went, of his most grandiose desire! The light was dropping, a quick reminder that our time was done: "Yes, that always was your trouble," I sang out, as if in pain.

Today, a little heavier over the flagstones of Europe, Tom would not remember such a tale. I do not think it could belong to his current perception of the tangibility of things, which rushes him remorselessly from action into action. In any case, he sounds older now whenever—infrequently— we speak on the telephone. Is that the voice, I think, behind those thousand launchings, whose ten-year vessels cannot see that each conclusive horse is as bellied as himself and as prepared to pour out more and more? "I am sick," he said in self-remorse when he last spoke to me. "It clutches at my heart and does not let me move," he wailed; "It puts me out of pulse and frightens me." Ah god, I thought, the man is dying, dying of invention. This was in Paris, walking alone amid the sprinkling of sharp Western rain. But I knew it meant that had I in Bombay—leaving India in the opposite direction from the gateway that should have heralded me—

visited the Elephanta Caves, I knew already what I would have found. The wind would have whipped its warmth around the caves, emptying them of echo, and wrinkled out of sight across the flatness of that sea: all that would remain for me to hear would be the way one howled to the other, "Goodbye to the greatness of Tom!"

# THE RIGHT PATH; OR,
# THEY TOOK THE WRONG ROAD

It was when he was a nymphet of a lad, a silken-kneed slip in a uniform that included a turquoise turban every Tuesday and Thursday morning, that Shahid came back from Aitchison, his school, to tell us his teacher was writing a book about him. We were then living in the 44 B-2 house in Gulberg, I think built by a man who had a fish fetish: apart from the utterly unusable fish-shaped swimming pool in the back garden—an obvious advertisement of his need—there were ghostly fishes strewn all about the house, so that simply to contemplate doorknobs, or light fixtures, or even the proportions of a veranda would be to murmur, "fish." "A book!" said Ifat in massive disbelief, "But why?" It turned out that Shahid's Islamic studies teacher had walked up to him in the playground that morning, saying in kindly fashion, "Shahid, you are a very good boy. I am going to write a book about you." Then he had walked away. We were entranced, particularly when, a few months later, the Islamic studies teacher did indeed publish a book: it was a pale pink paperback, printed with economy—*The Right Path* it was called. But what had this to do with Shahid? The book taught a body how to pray, how to fast, how to do *wazzoo* (that is, how to ablute), and dressed perfectly respectable

Arabic words in Roman togs with a vaudeville sense of glee. It was, in short, a textbook, designed for schools such as ours that still taught in English and thus needed texts such as *The Right Path* to supply us with left-to-right pages on which we could exercise our ambidextrous eyes. When *The Right Path* came our way, however, Ifat and I devoured it less for Islam than for Shahid—but how hard we had to look for him! The virtue of those pages was beginning to depress us, when my eyes fell upon a chapter titled "Goodness!" "Let's take a look at that one," Ifat said, and turning to it, we read

> Shahid is a good boy.
> Shahid is a neat boy.
> Shahid is a clean boy.

It made us mirthful. "But Shahid," I spluttered when he came home from Aitchison that evening, "where's the plot?"

It came later, the plot, on a day when he returned home with all the urgency of one who carries crucial news. It was not my father he wanted, however, nor my mother: Shahid was looking for Ifat and for me. "Do you know what my Islamic studies teacher said today?" he demanded when he had found us. We did not. The teacher had said, "You used to be a good boy, but now you are a dog." We laughed at that, but it was not all, for he had also said, slowly and reproachfully, "Shahid, you are a scabble of a fish." A scabble of a fish! Ifat and I were thunderstruck. Was it open knowledge, then, the way we lived? Whence did that phrase originate? From a native strain of sticklebacks, maybe, those finny creatures who build nests? From an unknown Indian bastardy in which the guilty woman could only be Beatrix Potter? However hard we thought, we could not locate its parentage and, instead, ushered it into our vocabulary the way an orphan comes. "Oh, but he's awful, Shahid," I would say, twenty years later, "he's just a scabble of a fish." Even today, in the way days come and go, conglomerations of gray pigeons, I can still brush against a conversation where I hear a voice say, "But she's a scabble of a fish, and nothing else"—"Oh," I think, "I am standing in a room inhabited by a sometime friend of Shahid!"

I was born shortly after Shahid, a few days under fifteen months, which suggests that I did after all partake in some fashion of the scene I wish to envision. I am thinking of my mother at twenty-nine carrying Shahid at six months to see my father during the visiting hours of the Karachi jail. Throughout our childhood it was one of Papa's favorite stories, making him laugh and shake his head to remember how when he tried to hold Shahid, the baby would adamantly lunge for the bars, delighted to find such a comrade in his father, in a father-sized playpen. So my parents let Shahid climb and swing on the metal that defined their meeting place—he made a tremendous din, which later on my father would boisterously replicate in the continuous tense in which he framed his anecdotes: "I am trying to hug the monkey, but he just keeps climbing up and climbing up!" I was there all the time, fetally speaking, as a very carefully folded thought—Papa was in the Karachi jail for roughly the period of my gestation, in prison for sedition at that time. I must have heard my mother say that word a thousand times when I still had gills.

Poor Shahid, his babyhood must have felt quite cramped, flanked as he was by females, Ifat before him and me following so fast behind! It made him slightly forgetful as a child, ready to drop a curtsy on the wrong occasion, and earnest, always, when he was being teased. But still, I seem to remember being kind as well, taking him by the hand and leading him to my parents' room when he cried during the night, and being patient with his more silly games. So I feel perplexed today when during a discussion of our tribal ways, he can glance at me gloomily and say, "You engulfed my youth, the two of you." "But Shahid," I exclaim, "you were the apple of my eye when I was six!" "Isn't that enough?" he answers angrily. For after having been such a mild-mannered infant, Shahid has grown increasingly committed to the art of indignation, waking up in the morning with an expression of incipient disgust already in stock for all the affronts he will surely encounter during the course of the day. I certainly strike him as stupid: in my company, he continually has to keep glancing round at me just to check on whether he should be bridling at some fresh stupidity. When I last visited him in London, my heart sank to discover that the final front on which he had been prepared to acknowledge ignorance had fallen—Shahid had learned to cook. And when we were in the kitchen shortly thereafter I could see him watching me: "Is that the way you cut your onions?" he said, a man aghast. "Oh, you most overweaned and overweaning person!" I called out in reply.

But we were good friends when I was six, the family having moved by that time from the Fowler Lines house in Karachi to the 23-H Gulberg house in Lahore, and then to 9-T Gulberg, from where Papa went to jail, which moved us back to Karachi, and finally to London—so we were living in Chiswick, then, by the time Shahid was seven and I was six. His most cherished tale from that era puts us both in the playground on our first day of school, where he swears that I suddenly bent down, picked up a brick, and simply hurled it at him. "Little girls don't do things like that in this country," he tells me I was told. I, however, have no recollection of that moment: I wonder what I was thinking of, it makes me ask today. For I can distinctly recall what was in our minds when, three years earlier, on a holiday to England, some demon of merriment prompted us both to jump into the Serpentine. My parents were in France and had taken Ifat with them, leaving the two of us with my mother's father, an unsuspecting man. What astonishment we must have wrought upon him on the afternoon he took us to play in the park where, all of a sudden, those two brown little renditions of his flesh and blood tossed themselves into the Serpentine! "How can you be so naughty?" Mamma mourned when she returned.

After having lived in England for some years, we were accustomed to feeling foreign, which we felt just as strongly, in turn, when we went back to Pakistan. Lahore in June was hot, and in any case we were not the children anymore, that function having been taken over by Tillat and Irfan, the baby: we were somewhere else, and in-between. First we lived in Model Town, a former Sikh community on the outskirts of Lahore, where the houses were large and strange and painted peculiar colors. Ours was pale green and had a triangular lawn in front of it, lined with the tallest eucalyptus trees that I had ever seen. But we did not stay there long; the following year we were moving again, to a house on Mayo Road, which I recollect indelibly as the hapless pinnacle of my comradeship with Shahid. For little did we know, the first night we were there, that we had spread ourselves at the heart of hunting-cockroach land.

Having moved in that morning in normal disarray, it seemed easier at night to spread a sheet on the floor and sleep beneath the fan instead of bothering with beds—which is exactly what Shahid and I did. Halfway through the night, however, my dream began to tell me, "There is not just one but many things crawling on you." I woke in terror and plummeted into worse when I saw the floor around me black and seething with a sea of cockroach backs that glinted in the moonlight. "Shahid!" I whispered my scream, "look!" "Aaaah!" screamed Shahid. In a bound, dragging me in his tow, he was up on top of the bunk beds, where we sat horrified, marooned in movement. But the cockroaches sensed where we went and followed us, advancing with unified stealth, tracking us down. As a column of them came up over the top of the mattress, we had no choice but to leap from the bed onto a chest of drawers in the corner of the room; there our parents found us standing an hour later, arms around each other, weakly wailing, "Help!" It was enough to break my spirit for several days afterward, and I never did re-establish any trust with Mayo Road for as long as we lived in that house.

The following summer, before we moved into the 44 B-2 fish house, we went to the hills again, and it gladdened our eyes and our appetites to be back in Nathia Gali, that winsome Himalayan village. The Valley View Hotel was a funny place: it had enormous rooms into which clouds would float the first thing in the morning—we would wake up in that creaky wooden structure with them wafting round our beds. It made me curiously glad. I shared a room with Shahid, Ifat, and Nuz; we spent the days walking and talked into the night. The evening felt full of structure to me: after Irfan and Tillat had been put to bed in the little room adjoining my parents', Papa and Mamma would just want to sit and let Papa talk politics, while the four of us went off to the dining room to eat hugely and to chat. What delight we derived from a fellow guest of the hotel who seemed to eat at exactly the same time that we did! He was a somber-looking man, always alone, who at the end of every meal would pick up his napkin with solemnity and emphasis thereby to blow his nose. That anticipated punctuation caused us considerable glee, until one day Nuz—seeking to restrain us—hissed, "Stop it! Think of something sad!" "That poor man," I said in a minute, "has a cold." Odd, to think that such a silly thing could reduce us into carnival. Odd, that that year, 1965, was the last time the four of us ever congregated in a room.

A person most happy in our happiness at vacationing in the hills was Master Sahib, the Urdu tutor my father had procured for me to share with Shahid. Master Sahib would come striding down Mayo Road, always in native clothes, always carrying an umbrella, which he deployed as a walking stick. Papa complained that he used us to practice his English rather than to teach us Urdu, but we loved him anyway. He had a white beard and a certain little beam, which, when I first noticed it, made me think to myself, "Oh, now I understand what books mean when they talk of people with twinkles in their eyes." "You are in a jovial mood, Shahid," Master Sahib would say, "do you intend to encroach on Sara's time?" For he would drink tea in between Shahid's lesson and mine, pulling out of his waistcoat pocket a small bag of confectionery, which he enjoyed greatly, as he slurped his tea. "Ah!" he exclaimed one afternoon, shortly before we left for the hills, "your mother is at her organ once again!" Shahid and I looked down, embarrassed, since Mamma was playing the piano. "She must take her organ with her when she goes," declared Master Sahib, enjoyment reaching all the creases of his face, "how it would resound across the valleys!" I stared down at my Urdu book and then up at him. "Yes," I weakly said.

Were we on the right path then, I wonder, or were we off? It felt hard, of course, in the September of that year, when Pakistan and India went to war for some twelve days and my parents, for safety's sake, shipped their first three children out of Lahore and off to Campbellpur. Campbellpur, a city without sewers, was too nondescript a place to have warranted a name change in the way that Lyallpur was transformed into Faisalabad and all those towns named after British generals with "pur" tagged on as a suffix turned—after 1947—radically native in their names. But I am talking of 1965, when Ifat and Shahid and I found ourselves suddenly in Campbellpur, a nonentity of a place somewhere in the North Punjabi regions: a safe city, but one without sewers. Something veered away from us at that point, I recall, because once we were gathered back in Rawalpindi that winter—we had moved again—the structure of a day felt different, as though the transition from morning into afternoon had suddenly become a dislocated thing, filling us with unease. Our paths did not converge with their former regularity; they matched instead the new terrain on which we lived, the dissected plateau of the Pothwar. After Lahore, Rawalpindi hardly felt like a town at all, pleasing us only in its environs: there were manic rock formations—old structures, troubling—to which we would drive in the evenings, and then the Margalla Hills, the horizon's constant. Ifat missed Lahore: she returned there for college and got married too, urging us all into a consciousness of reconfiguration. Shahid became a brooding boy, and we hardly spoke at all.

That was the year Tillat came to me, her heart shaken,

97

and breathed out, "Sara, have you ever read, *They Took the Wrong Road?*" I was her stern elder in those days, and she did not trust me much, so she must have felt considerable distress to appeal to me thus. I had read *They Took the Wrong Road*, at about her age, when I was eight and equally vulnerable to that vicious little tale. The story is ostensibly for children, but written out of the most malignant motive, telling a cautionary story of how Mummy explains to Bessie and John why a mother could end up starving her son or a father killing his daughter. It all begins, says Mummy calmly, when they are little, and a little girl—like you, Bessie—carelessly forgets to feed her pet hamster and takes the wrong road; or a little boy like John punches his baby sister in a naughty game, and he takes the wrong road. What Mummy proceeds to list as the basis of all violent crime were the kind of activities that I engaged in several times a day, and I did not like her logic. Tillat didn't either. It seemed rather hard, she pointed out, that the little girl is both the one who gets killed and the one who gets the blame for it. "It's just written by someone who believes that it's better to be the bathwater than the baby," I told her consolingly.

But where was Shahid in those years? I can picture what he looked like in that time, but I certainly could not guess at what that face was thinking. I was now the eldest daughter in the house, and my duties had doubled, so perhaps that contributed to sending him to the periphery, to reading history or running off to live in the Margalla Hills. He did not spend much time with us, joining in our conversations barely long enough to make Mamma laugh in the way that only he could do. Or he would play with Tillat and Irfan, making them run maniacally complicated races all around the house, their babyhood panting and sweating in the course of his agon. While I worked inside with Mamma, copying out Papa's articles or marking papers, we could hear in the garden his perpetual yell, "Tillat and Irfan, you are both baboons!—No you're not—you're like spoon, like baboon!" For those several years, he and I lived in different realms, suspending any ordinary commerce of conversation. On occasional grounds, of course, we would encounter: there was a brief spate of chess playing, I remember, one winter, and then there also was Chishti.

Chishti Sahib was a dapper-looking man. From his moderate demeanor no one would have guessed at all the pedagogical frenzy he carried on his back, as densely packed as the hump of a camel. I do not even think he was fully aware of it himself, so at this moment he would probably be most put out of step to know that, if we could meet him, both Shahid and I would take his hand in celebration, saying, "You have changed my life." Chishti was the last in a long line of Urdu tutors who straggled into the house to teach us Urdu; some of them were very peculiar people, and I do not recall doing much learning until Chishti came our way. For Chishti gave us the ghazal. Until that time we had only perfunctory acquaintance with that rare breed of poem, conceiving of it as the kind of writing that someone like my father would resort to when he was in his most declarative mood. But Chishti changed that for us, filling our brains with a mathematical ingenuity that felt heady as incense. "It's like geometry—no, it's relativity," we breathed, in wonder that our faulty discourse had not noticed this before. Chishti's face would transform at the thought of a verse, and we, spellbound, could only follow the lineaments of his expression as it coaxed us in precarious veers up to the vertiginous idiom of Mīrzā Asadullāh Khān Ghālib. That master poet of Delhi wrote at the court of the last Mughal emperor and, after the Mutiny of 1857, mourned fiercely for the demise of the city he had known. Mīrzā Sahib, my salaam to you.

I did, in recent days, pay my respects to Ghālib, stopping in at the Ghālib Academy in the Nizamuddin section of Delhi. Upstairs in the academy there is a library and a museum: it soothed me to be there, laying a finger on those old spines, bending over those faded letters. Then, to my surprise, I noticed that half the museum was given over to an exhibition called "The Foods Ghālib Liked to Eat." That musty glass case had obviously been there for years, with its array of wax mangoes, and chicken stuffed with saffron, and even a lamb chop. "What an amazing idea," I thought, "what a wonderful thing to do for a poet!" Ghālib, a mischievous man, would have been amused, I felt sure; but I also felt sure that I had hit upon the perfect present for Shahid. One year, for his birthday, I could just give him a glass box entitled "Foods That Ghālib Liked to Eat." It would rapidly assume pride of place, I know, in that boy's gypsy home.

Close on twenty years later, Chishti still crops up in our conversation as someone we like to name, just as we like to quote what we remember of Ghālib back and forth to one another, shaking our heads all the while. "Urdu is the only poetry for me," Shahid declared to me fastidiously after such a session. We were sitting in his peculiar bank flat in Connaught Square shortly after his wife had left him. "Really?" I responded, wonderingly. "Yes." And then, happy to be shadowboxing and to jab a bit at me, "I could never take to English!" he added jauntily. I thought about that, and about how I could, until some sullen principle of honesty prompted him to mutter, "except for 'Christabel.'" "For what?" I asked, amazed at his capacity to surprise me, "For 'Christabel'?" "Yes!" His face lit up with recollection. "Mamma taught it to me, you know," he mused. "Mamma taught me 'Christabel.'" Heartsore, he could not help but sigh,

> Jesu Maria, shield her well,
> Hush, beating heart of Christabel!

"I have never heard a lovelier thing," he gravely said. I was silent then, but later in the night I think I heard again,

> Jesu Maria, shield her well,
> Hush, beating heart of Christabel!

But that was years later, in recent times, long after I awoke at eighteen ready to be friends again with Shahid, only to find him gone. We had always thought of him, having as he did the greater mobility of the male, as the most Pakistani of us: it never crossed my mind that he would choose to stay away or choose a life that would not allow him to return. But then I had been so busy working for Pip that I had not stopped to consider what it must have been like to live in his house and not work for him, that it might well have sent one to the periphery, perhaps, or to the hills. For although Papa and Shahid always regarded each other's minds with keen respect, they were both people of well-formed opinion, and there were a couple of subjects over which they tended to clash. They clashed over history and over womankind. It took me years to realize it: what else was Shahid doing in the years of his retreat but putting fresh air in between himself and Pip's tyrannical dependence on history and on women? My brother must have thought we were at fault as well, we family women who let ourselves be so put upon, leaving our possible rebellion like ghosts in every room.

Shortly before Shahid went to England, we moved back to Lahore, shifting house in the December of the 1971 war with India, this time to Zafar Ali Road. For the next five years we actually kept on living there, the longest period we stayed in a single space, a span of time in which my life showed signs of taking shape again after years of feeling formless. "What a relief it is to see Sara becoming nice at last," I heard Ifat tell my mother, "for a while she was quite difficult." "Difficult is as difficult does," I added, meaningfully, since we had seen a regrouping once again, a shift in tone that made new allegiances available to us. Tillat was adding herself to our circle, and Ifat living in the same city, so for a second time there were three of us—a brightening thought for me.

After Shahid left, our paths didn't cross for years, and I had no notion of whether Shahid was driving up the wrong road or how he planned to plot out his next move. I missed, however, the aesthetic of his face—his eyes, their lag of lid—using it as a talisman of sorts when I too sat down at the map to wonder what came next. Despite the proliferating duties of my day I knew at last that my time in Lahore was done: I spent many hours pondering over possible routes, until the quickest way from here to . . . what? formed itself as my most efficient question. I had a dread that a creeping laziness of soul would make me sink into the first chair that I found—preferably a comfortable chair, but the first one that I found. "You can always just go, you know," Tillat pointed out, "and then decide later." "That's what Shahid did," I said. It struck me suddenly that all of us might well be equipped with a deep-seated, chartless frivolity, something that sent us dressing ourselves in ostrich feathers well beyond our time, as though we were designed to follow curvations of such sandy monsters—"That would be terrible, terrible!" I exclaimed. "Well, we grew up with a terrible need for history and women," Tillat quite soberly replied.

There is a Safeway on the outskirts of Kuwait. It sits alone beyond the fifth ring road, those massive highways that curl around the shopping centers of that town, which also constitute the country. Standing outside that Safeway in the white heat was deranging, syncopating vague impressions of Kuwait—a place I didn't know—with something I knew quite well but in a different space. I was tired from a recent trip, and "Where were we all, where were we all?" it made me keep repeating. Later, in the car, I murmured to my brother-in-law, "These ring roads are a very good idea: at least you can never say, 'They Took the Wrong Road.'" Then I burst into a clatter of laughter; Farooq was impeccably polite, but "What a peculiar woman she is," I could see him thinking. Shahid has never visited Tillat in Kuwait. He came to see me once in Williamstown, but he has never visited me in New Haven, city of the hunted eyes.

I could not lay my finger on it at first when I moved to New Haven, but I knew that a trouble sat on every conversation that I had, and it vexed me to be ignorant. Then one day I realized, why, there are rabbits in everybody's eyes, creatures who in panic dart around with all the agility of things that can be hurt! No one, from the youngest to the oldest person here, seemed exempt from that flickering of vision; with a sigh I knew that I now lived in a world where every conversation threatened to construe itself into a judgment of the soul. For a talking woman, it felt hard, at first, to have so many whites of eye in mind that seemed to protect themselves in the wrong direction, veering into publicity of their need. I grew used to it, though, and now when my friends shake their heads and groan, "Oh, university!"—I answer briskly, "Rubbish! It's the fault of living in this ugly city and its evil climate."

But I was not living in New Haven when my mother died—that happened during the first few years of my American retreat. And so it was that when I next saw Shahid, we had lost the chance to gauge in ordinary ways each other's timbre as a friend, for our bond had suffered change. Shahid's face looked older, his eyes haunted by a sense that it had been error to have put all his loyalty into one basket and to have saved no more significant time for friendship with his mother, whom he loved. It was hard, in consequence, to determine whose dues were getting settled when we met in that complicated system of debt. I had not gone home for her funeral and needed a fund of stories told me to acclimatize my mind to the turns of that strange plot. So Shahid talked to me out of a wealth of incongruity, bringing me to the point where I could stop with recognition and say yes to the familiar detail of it all, like Nuzzi's laugh. Nuzzi laughs wonderfully, like little pebbles clattering in a rusty can: "clatter, clatter, clatter," laughs Nuz. I heard those stories and felt curiously reassured, needing for Shahid to repeat them: it was not fair, I knew, but when we met, I needed him to talk to me as from a wellspring of euphoria.

Henceforth we met in gentler times. (For in this story, Ifat will not die before our eyes: it could not be countenanced. How could I tell Shahid's story and let Ifat die before his eyes? Have I nothing in me, then, to intervene between him and that great indelicacy? So we will say nothing of the time when Shahid told me, "We are lost, Sara," and "Yes, Shahid, we are lost," I firmly said.) It was as though we had reorganized our municipalities, or a large-spirited mayor in New Haven had suddenly done away with all those one-way streets, allowing us to meet at last on dual carriages. Perhaps someone in Lahore had also eased the traffic of its crazy streets by banning horse-drawn tongas from the roads, soothing Ifat's soul. She hated the one that carried her daily from Queen Mary's, our school, back to Mayo Road— cocky, stalky thing that she was then, how it made her crimson with scorn!

They have never blushed in regular ways, not during all the years I've known them. Embarrassment or shame seem to command more rarefied techniques upon their change- ability of face, as if to contemplate their expression is to say, firmly, no. So Ifat blushed with outrage and then would blanch with scorn; Shahid blushes with fierce indignation; Tillat turns red with rage. Nuzzi I think tinges slightly when she laughs, but then she and I as the darker sisters always faced the world with that extra bonus, a pigmented veil. "Who would have thought, Shahid," I said delicately, as we walked arm in arm through London, "that you would end up working in a bank?" "I wouldn't," he said. And then, picking up my gauntlet, "When you left Pakistan those years ago, was teaching English what you thought you'd want?" "Never!"— I was extravagant—"I thought I had served my time and the world was curling with pleasure at the thought of taking care of me!" We curved across a street that shone with rain. "But then who would have thought of Tillat," I added, "as a baby factory?" "I would!" "Really?" I wondered, glancing up at him, "Somehow the only one of us who made sense to me was Irfani, biting his lip at the crossroads and finally decid- ing, 'I'll take the one that's wrong!'" Shahid laughed at this, his face softening at last, and deeply pleasing me.

For yes, of course, there is history for us in England, but certainly not of the press-clanking, deadline-demanding sort that kept us trotting from town to town throughout our childhood to the extent that not one of us today would ever claim we miss the texture of newsprint. But the hurly-burly of it all? Now that's a different issue, for the trouble with hurly-burly is that it can feel convincing, as though you were always residing in what Papa used to call the fact of the matter, never nuanced, never on the periphery of things. "To walk away from such a history is all very well," I pointed out to Shahid, "but it is less easy to walk away from that other thing, from womankind." It made us realize that Papa was more wily than we thought when he constructed his terrible dependencies, always leaving himself room to move from one thing to the other. "But you did no wrong, no wrong," I reassured him, "to have thus eliminated option from your life: what choice did you have but to walk away from history, and practice at the gentleness of hands?"

"And you?" he said to me. I sighed. Then we both set about brightening our conversation, in a sudden surge of practicality, like the one that allows you to get up at last and empty out the ashtray, put order to a room. "You were always stupid," he said meditatively, "and of us all, clearly the one most mad . . ." But the "but" in his voice refused to take further shape. I had always liked it when he called me stupid; and I thought how comforting it was to grow old with Shahid, walking over the creases of those old comparisons: we had shared them since our first tadpole flailings. "Remember," I said warningly, "that I've lived many years as an otherness machine, had more than my fair share of being other, so if my brother or my father start picking up on the trend, I have every right to expostulate!" He laughed. Then, made hungry and thirsty by too much talk, we set off to put food back at the center of things.

I was not surprised but his friends were confounded when, some years earlier, Shahid at such a young age chose to get married, have children, and settle down. "That brilliant boy," said Jamie in disgust, "who could have done anything!" He fastidiously proceeded to wash his hands of Shahid, transferring in a courtly way to me his quota of affection. Now he is my friend rather than my brother's, but somehow in the tenderness of his regard I think I can detect him looking at me as though at the grave of that brilliant boy. "Who could want to live on the fringes?" Jamie muttered, and I found it impossible to explain the lambent quality of the periphery, its curious sense of space. "Oh, life must be at a really low ebb if you need concealed lighting to make it interesting," I murmured inconsequentially.

So I was not surprised but merely sorrowful to see the reparation in Shahid's eye as he fed and clothed his daughter. It seemed dangerous to me: how many things could be set right, I thought, in one stroke of the hand? But Shahid has always been interested in reparation, ever since the days his inspiration failed him when we sat down to make those obligatory birthday cards for our parents. It was Ifat's idea, of course—she could never rest until she had urged us on to more invention. But Shahid's inspiration failed, so that all he could draw was a little stickman, adding inside, as a happy afterthought, "Sorry it's such a rotten card, but I wish you a very kind regard!" His policy was that if he could not make cards then at least he could make amends: residues of that innocence still quicken his heart today.

But how can I pick up on that *Right Path* lingo, listing all the things that Shahid should or should not have done, different ways he could have plotted out his necessary mistakes? His trouble now, he readily admits, is that he has fallen into the habit of fidelity, which I tell him is the worst addiction of them all, most difficult to break. Since all roads lead to habit in the end, I suppose it hardly makes a difference, the route one chooses—or wills not to choose—on which to arrive. Nevertheless, whether he breaks or makes amends with habit, I conjure him to remember the significant labor he performed when he maintained, through all those years, his astonishing gaiety of soul. "It's not frivolity," I urged him, "it's work—painstaking, extravagant work!" "We can't be spendthrift all the time," he replied in reprimand.

Once, on a hot afternoon at the 44 B-2 Gulberg fish house in Lahore, Papa surprised us by coming home unexpectedly—we had thought he was out of the town—with a steaming basket of fish from Bhatti Gate, always a delectable meal. We ate with festivity, for he was hugely satisfied to see his family eat, and none of us could resist the great white flakes of that Rao fish, caught freshly from the Ravi and then cooked at Bhatti Gate in a red batter that hours later would still tingle at the lips. Later, as though he had suddenly hit upon the next twist of a narrative, Shahid came in search of Ifat and me and suggested, "Let's fill up the fish!" It took us a second to realize that he was talking about the swimming pool, over which we had expended frequent laughter, that lay, consuming useless space, in the farther corner of the garden. "But why?" demanded Ifat, from her bed. "So we can swim in it, of course!" Then he added, cajolingly, "Think how happy it would make the man with the fetish!" But Ifat was adamant; she was supine. "Do you think I would put my body in that thing?" she asked, aghast. "No, I would feel too ridiculous"—she lay back again, white arm across her face. Shahid looked at her a moment and then turned to lesser pleas: "But you will, Sara, won't you? Come on, rally round!" He appealed to a phrase to which I had commitment, and so I rallied round.

The pool first needed to be cleaned, and the sun at four was blisteringly hot as we went about looking for the necessary accoutrements. "Children, don't get heatstroke!" my mother called out warningly. But shortly we had clambered down onto its gritty surface, where all I seemed to find were scorpion skeletons, and lizards darting across my singed feet. "There are scabbles at the bottom of this fish, Shahid!" I cried out in dismay. "Never mind, Sara," he said soothingly, "think what fun it's going to be!" I felt doubtful; still, we cleaned and cleaned, sweat trickling from my skull all down my neck, mimicking the shivering course of some unknown insect. It was dusk when we were done and could finally turn on the taps to fill the fish. After a slightly acrid hiss, a reticent and pale brown water began to gush into the pool. We sat watching it, our legs dangling over the side, until I thought it necessary to say to him, "It is a fish of great depth, Shahid. Let's give up." I think he would have agreed, had not Ifat stepped out at that moment to laugh at us her lovely jeering laugh. It confirmed his purpose: "Give the fish some patience," Shahid insisted to me.

By the time we were cavorting in that water, with voices of a people who had earned the right to slippery glee, it was dark around us, dark enough for me not to notice all the impact to my skin when I, leaning back to laugh, made contact with that surface. The others, standing around in the garden among the fireflies, came out to laugh as well, so it was only the following morning that I looked down to notice all those tiny abrasions that had closed like secrets in the night. "Look what you did to me," I said reproachfully over breakfast, displaying as I could not help but do the tiny writing on my skin. "I am so sorry!" Shahid exclaimed, and put an arm about me. "I had not meant it to hurt, but just for us to have some fun!" "It doesn't matter," I said gloomily, and kissed him. "It never had a plot to it, anyway, the story of your goodness."

# PAPA AND PAKISTAN

There were always a few words that his flamboyant English insisted he mispronounce: words, I often imagined, over which his heart took hidden pleasure when he had got them by the gullet and held them there until they empurpled to the color of his own indignant nature. "Another" was one of them—I cannot count how many times each day we would hear him say, "Anther?" "Anther?" It did not matter whether it was another meal or another government or another baby at issue: all we heard was a voice bristling over with amazement at the thought that anther could exist. It seemed his patience could not sustain itself over the trisyllabic, tripping up his voice on most trisyllables that did not sound like "Pakistan"—for there was a word over which he could slow down, to exude ownership as he uttered it! But something like "beginning"—that is, something more mundane—had to become "bigning," a hasty abbreviation that was secretly aware of the comic quality of slapdash, the shorthand through which slapdash begins. He was a journalist, after all. We of course could only listen, with loyal cells producing their precious moisture almost at the pace at which that large voice was speaking, suspecting itself, and then dismissing suspicion to talk on and on. How was it possible for us, chosen audience of those locutions, not to listen with our spirits on our lips, thrilling with compassion? It was not possible, and told us of the way our days designed themselves to be. For in the bigning, there was Pip.

They must have hit upon their names in about the same era, that decade of the 1930s, when Ziauddin Ahmed—a Rajput Salahria, employee of the imperial government in India—decided to become Z. A. Suleri the writer, and some Indian Muslims in England decided it was high time to talk about Islamic independence and invented that new coinage, Pakistan. The word emerged from Cambridge, actually, where a group of three students published a small pamphlet entitled "Now or Never," followed by the winning subtitle "Are We to Live or Perish Forever?" It always struck me as a particularly Pakistani question, combining as it did the obvious with umbrage and ignoring the fact that "now" is a tricky word, embedded in the oblique. At the time of its publication Papa must have moved to Delhi to live with his aunt after his father died: there he became a civil servant, and how his spirit chafed at the recollection of those days! He would get up in the morning in despair, thinking of all the other mornings he would also have to rise, take the same road to the same office, and look forward to nothing more than coming home again. "Was that to be the compass of my life?" he thundered, glaring at me as though I were at least the aunty who had conjured him to remain in such respectable employ. I did not deserve his glare, for my spirit quite cheered at the thought of him giving up his job and writing poems and, with his cousin Shamim, peddling film scripts all the way from Delhi to Bombay. But Pip was always a wonderful consumer of context: he would eat it up alive, just like a cannibal, so no audience that came his way departed without feeling slightly stripped. It was hardly simple, playing the part of never to his now, but then which good humor would not soften at the manifest satisfaction with which he ate?

He ate up his past, too, in the manner of a nervous eater,

so that my attempts to establish some sense of the narrative of his days always filled me with a sense of uneasy location. There were some stories he told wonderfully, and we were trotted over them with all the expansiveness of people who conglomerate for the exclusive joy of traversing, once again, familiar terrain. But establishing the sequence of those stories was a less easy thing to do, and for some years I would chide myself for owning an absentminded brain, a faculty so distracted that it could not even retain the structure of my father's life as part of its water table's constant. But then I noticed all the detail he had to forget in order to pay vociferous attention to his now, and saw that it was not my proper task to be divining out the silence of his streams. Still, he could surprise me. "Mamma," I asked once, after an evening filled with his wonderful stories, "why does Papa call his grandmother his 'elder mother'?" A quick change of manner crossed her face. "Oh, my dear," she said slowly, "he isn't talking about his grandmother: he's talking about his father's other wife." I realized then that there would always be mirages in his eyes for me, who had no way of knowing all the ground he must have covered to domesticate his life.

My Dadi should have given me a clue, of course. But she, that most imperious soul, was not a woman much given to intimate chitchat, far preferring to praise God or curse men instead. She came from Meerut—heart of Urdu-speaking land—and was somehow married to my grandfather, a Punjabi Rajput from Sialkot who evidently had several wives. His name was Karim Baksh, and I have never quite deciphered what he actually did to keep himself employed. And so we would question Siraj Din, a relative from my grandfather's village, when he came up to visit us in Lahore; but Siraj Din was no help at all. "Oh, he was very pious," he assured us solemnly, "a very pious man." I further gleaned that he was fond of traveling, and, in the last quarter of the last century went all the way to Mecca to do as a Muslim should his Hajj, returning to have the first brick mosque built in his Sialkot village—Deovli, it is called. Then he spent much time in the princedoms of Deccan, that region of India slightly south of the north, and my father told me stories of all that he would and would not do when he visited him as a child in the princely houses. Beyond that, however, I cannot imagine what my grandfather did, apart from having several wives. "He loved to ride camels!" Papa once said, appreciatively, at which point I just gave up. "Wait! My grandfather," I said steadily, "was fifty years old when he married that slip of a thing, my Dadi at sixteen, his second wife. Beyond that, he liked to ride camels—am I right?" Papa looked up, surprised at such unnecessary interruption: "Why, yes!" he simply said.

But when was Pip in one place long enough for us to walk over him scientifically, his past our archaeological site? If anything, he was in too many places at once, recounting different histories for each, which overwhelmed us with the clamor they made for his complete attention. And I have no reason to believe that he was ever different, even in the era of his youth when he decided that his life must write. So he moved from Delhi to Lahore and went back to the university, earning one degree in Persian and anther in journalism, torn as he was between the literary and the political, uncertain on which to land. In later years he would tell me with a sigh, "I did myself disservice when I gave up my tongue." But a young man of his times hardly had a choice when he found himself seduced by history but to give up Urdu or Hindi in the service of English, which was history's language then. Generations of Urdu conversation in his genes must have shuddered with desertion as Papa's imperatives sent him off, away from poetry, into an English daily. He adopted it with a Dickensian zeal, picking up phrases and tonalities that he would never lose: he always talked about newspapers as dailies, as morningers or eveningers, for "newspaper" was a reader's word. He was happy, then, feeling at the hub of himself and of history, and shortly thereafter was to feel happier still. For then he met Jinnah.

Consider Papa, growing up in a part of northern India

known as Quadian, born in 1913 when his father was approaching sixty, first seduced by poetry, and then by history. What else could he do when he met Jinnah but exclaim, "Amazing grace!" Jinnah was an actor, certainly the most aware of all the politicians of India at that time of how to maintain a poetical posture in its history. So Pip became a person swamped in the true devotion of his soul, working in the service of what he could only name perfection. And he named it, constantly: he saw to it that I grew up in a world that had only a single household god, called the Quaid, so that even today I feel slightly insolent to my upbringing when reality prompts me to call him by his real name, Jinnah. It is a curious epithet, the Quaid, that—after he had manhandled the country into being—Pakistan adopted to call the Leader, but in our home that title conveyed an added twist, becoming in Pip's impassioned discourse nothing other than the Father. No wonder I never learned more details of my grandfather, I mused, when Papa had thus named the Quaid and then veered off into his rapturous litany of desire. But what an odd man to make familial: gaunt with elegance and intellect, the discourse of a barrister imprinted on his brain, Jinnah the maker of Pakistan was hardly an easy idea to domesticate—and yet Pippy did it. He loved everything about that man: his design, his phrase, his clothes.

At that point, Papa was married to Baji, Nuzzi's mother. She was his cousin, and since earliest recall—when they were running round in some infant game—he knew as he watched her gambols, "That cousin is my wife." For so it had been decreed, and their marriage must have been quite a celebratory event, although Pip has never described it to me. Baji was a child, my father twenty-five, when after college in Lyallpur he was married to her. The next year, Nuz was born: they were such impassioned days for Pip that he could only name his daughter Nuzhat Shelley Suleri, to mediate between his inchoate regard for her and for Percy Bysshe. It made us weep with laughter when, decades later, Nuz confessed to us how she had been named: no wonder you are such a comic spirit, we told her, for how could a life abstain from comedy after having its middle name signed over to Percy Bysshe? Baji must have been tolerant in those days to have allowed her baby to carry such a name, and Nuz strong to sustain her birthing and the events that followed shortly after. Indeed so, since the next year was the year of the Lahore Resolution.

When at the beginning of the century Jinnah turned from law to politics, the modernity of his mind naturally inclined him into becoming—as he was called—the Ambassador of Hindu-Muslim Unity. But the logic of arguing for independence unleashed odd thoughts in India, so that in 1930 the poet Iqbāl's Allahabad Address to the Muslim League could contain visionary references to the idea of a separate Indian Muslim nation. Jinnah was more pragmatic, however, when he turned to that opinion. "To me, Hindus, Muslims, Parsis, Harijans are all alike," Gandhi declared, "I cannot be frivolous when I talk of Quaid-i-Azam Jinnah. He is my brother." "The only difference is this," Jinnah replied, "that brother Gandhi has three votes and I have only one vote." It was that imbalance in parity which lead, in 1940, to the Lahore Resolution, when the Muslim League met in Lahore on the twenty-third of March and drafted the Pakistan Declaration. What a strange occasion it must have been: crowds of hundreds of thousands gathering in the open field next to the Badshahi Mosque, of which how many understood the two-hour speech that Jinnah rose to give, prefaced with the calm disclaimer, "The world is watching us, so let me have your permisssion to have my say in English"? "It has always been taken for granted that the Mussalmans are a minority, and we have got used to it for such a long time that these settled notions sometimes are very difficult to remove," Jinnah told that crowd in Lahore. "The Mussalmans are not a minority. The Mussalmans are a nation by any definition." Papa was in that crowd, of course, listening rapturously.

So, freshly fathered, Papa moved to Karachi in 1941 to join the weekly *Dawn* as a subeditor until it became a daily in

1943. Then he went to Lahore and the *Orient Press* as its Lahore editor: in that year, 1944, he wrote his first book, *The Road to Peace and Pakistan*. The next year, he wrote anther. Called *My Leader*, it combined a certain Carlylian hero-worship with an intuitively shrewd sense of political pragmatics. The book gave Pip some fame, but—even more—it gave him what in the years of my formation was referred to only as "the Letter": to this day it remains the one object in Pip's home that he has ever loved. "It is very encouraging to me indeed," Jinnah wrote, "that a man like you should have such a warm and affectionate corner for me." ("If this is a corner," I interpolated to Ifat, "what on earth does the center look like?") "I congratulate you on marshalling facts so well and giving a clear picture of the seven years of our struggle." Years later, I would think reproachfully about that phrase and the ideas it put into Papa's head, because he has been martialing facts ever since. He would forget that we weren't facts and would martial us too, up and down the nation.

The royalties from *My Leader* gave Papa an idea: he would go to England and propagate what he called the Pakistan Cause in the capitals of Europe. He went to Bombay to get Jinnah's blessing, and in 1945 bought a passage to England. He left Baji and Nuz with Baji's parents, and then he set sail. It must have been strange for him, arriving alone in London, learning the lay of another land: "I spent most of the day around Whitehall," he wrote years later, "attending briefings and press conferences in the Foreign and Commonwealth offices and in the lobbies of the House of Commons. At that time, I was the lone 'Pakistani' correspondent in Britain—'Pakistani' before Pakistan, because I didn't attend any of these gatherings without raising the issue of the Muslim struggle for Pakistan." I believe it, when I read it; it has the ring of veracity, particularly when his next sentence swerves off to add, in his charming fashion, "In my one unchanging blue suit I became a familiar figure among the journalists and politicians, and my busy-bee movements galled the bulging band of my Hindu counterparts, who had monopolized the scene for decades." But Papa could not have been at Whitehall all the time, for the next year he met my mother.

How could he do it, be so absentminded as to forget he already had a wife and daughter? There was always an alacrity to his switch of allegiance, but at least Karim Baksh was in his grave when Jinnah superseded him. They talked well together, it seems—Mamma at twenty-five must have been a talking thing—but I would hardly have thought that sufficient for him to pick up ten years of his life with Baji and just put it in his pocket. Oh, knowing his makeup I have no doubt he sang with pain, but he went through with it anyway. The divorce was conducted by mail, and in Karachi Nuz at nine was told that her grandparents were her parents, that Baji was her sister. You, Nuz, you knew that falsehood signified a grave composure: you took that gravity and worked upright to build on it the clarity of your smile, your laugh.

But 1947 saw another break: the break of Britain leaving the shores of India, that place of many countries, many people, which they had just tidied in two! In London, Papa pulled out his Muslim League flag and at some public ceremony was asked to unfurl it, giving him what he later called the most moving moment of his life. Today I often regret that he was not in Pakistan at the time of the partition, to witness those bewildered streams of people pouring over one brand-new border into another, hurting as they ran. It was extravagant, history's wrenching price: farmers, villagers, living in some other world, one day awoke to find they no longer inhabited familiar homes but that most modern thing, a Muslim or a Hindu nation. There was death and panic in the cities when they rose up to flee, the Muslims traveling in one direction, the Hindus in the other. I wish, today, that Pip had been a witness of it all: surely that would have given him pause and conferred the blessing of doubt? But he was still in postwar London, living with my mother now, although Baji may well have been a semblance of the question in his head when he sat down to write *Whither Pakistan?* Mamma says that Papa wept the following year, when Jinnah died. I am sure that he wept every day for that fund of free-floating worship in his soul until, in 1949, Mamma gave birth to Ifat.

What followed were the days of information, times so hectic that my mind tires in advance at the prospect of type-setting them. My parents returned to Karachi, with Ifat the object of their delight, but they returned to the absence of relatives in a culture studiously conscious of the posture of relation. Mamma was probably still too new, too puzzled, to notice it, but Pip must have uttered a great good-bye to the extended family of Pakistan before he cast himself with re-newed ferocity into the printing of its news. It was as though his life were determined to be as novel as the nation, so he started a new newspaper, the *Evening Times*. For the next several years Pip kept himself preoccupied by inventing newspapers and procreating: Shahid was born in the year that the *Evening Times* became a morninger; the *Times of Ka-rachi* and I followed close behind. By this time I know my mother must have had an inkling of it all, but she loved her babies and didn't seem to mind. I wish I had been there, however, or in a state of greater consciousness, on the occa-sion of Nuzzi's first visit to us, when, turning to my father, "Sir, you have such beautiful babies!" she exclaimed. She and Mamma regarded one another sorrowfully, Nuz tells me, and then without a word decided to convert into a shared responsibility their portions of guilt and loss. I can attest they were each other's closest friends in the years I grew up with Ifat and Shahid.

What sounds of conversation filled my infancy, patterns of urgent and perpetual talk! I heard my parents talking to each other all the time, but never of themselves, only about newspapers and circulations and odd names like Khwaja Nazimuddin and Mr. Liaquat Ali. For there was still a parlia-ment in Pakistan: an abundant, talk-filled era, long before we had developed with such gusto our taste for censorship and martial law. So prime ministers came and went, and Pip was in and out of jail: it made Ifat sob dramatically, "Oh, no, no, he's not a jailbird, not Papa!" But life had a center, like a printing press, constantly in motion. So when Papa was jailed for sedition, during my gestation, and Mamma was in charge of the *Times of Karachi*, she made her protest known. She ordered into press an empty paper, sheafs of blank newsprint that bore nothing but the title, the *Times of Karachi* and the burden of nude paper. Karachi citizens must have been left quite perplexed, picking up their papers on the following morning and finding nothing but barren newsprint. "She made them know how angry she was when she turned censorship into sedition!" Papa would exclaim in later years, gazing at his wife in proud regard, "Her drama added six months to my sentence!" Then he was in jail for what felt like the longest time for me, after we had moved to Lahore and Pip was imprisoned for the Gurmani case. It was either for libel or sedition—one of those words that possessed our infant imaginations—so that it did not matter to me that I had no idea who Gurmani was when Ifat and Shahid and I sat down to draw hideously vicious little representations of the man and send them off to Papa to cheer him up in jail.

I missed him when he was gone. But Papa's delight in his babies often implied that they were a respite after he had dealt with the day's true significance. As a result we stood like curious animals, urging one another to step forward in examination, to stalk round and to sniff the great machine at the heart of things from which we were a respite. It had a manufacturer's name emblazoned on one side: when we learned how to read, we bent down and spelled out "h-i-s-t-o-r-y." That was the author of it all, we thought, when Pip emerged from jail and found General Ayub in charge, the parliament disbanded: it made him decide that he had had his fill of editing for a while and should look for something different. So he became a foreign correspondent once again and shipped us off to England. Before we left, Mamma had another child, a little girl called Tillat, whose vastness of eye and absence of nose entranced us all, although Mamma was getting fatigued.

Papa felt odd about living in England, as though he were a minority once more, a person absented from the functioning of what he himself had built. He wrote, however, with a ferocity of soul, sending off dispatch after dispatch, so that in place of the clanking of a printing press the music of our day changed to Papa on the telephone: "R Robert, F Edward, D Dover," he would shout to some long-suffering telegraph service. And he wrote another book, called *Pakistan's Lost Years*, for he was developing a glimmering fear that perhaps the country would completely forget what it means to be historical. I think Pip feared for his progeny as well. One day he glanced up from his work to stare at Ifat intently, who was at that phase in life when being stared at is dangerous. We were growing, he noticed, into a dangerous phase—what choice had he but to make Mamma pack our bags again and return to Pakistan, to forestall us lest we become totally possessed by someone else's history? Before we left, Irfan was born. My mother was very fatigued.

Pakistan had changed during General Ayub's Decade of Development, which was still in full swing when we returned. There was more of the army in the air, of course, more uniformity around to censor discourse. So many newspapers had been nationalized that to be an editor was tantamount to working for the government. Papa's spirit rose up in rebellion at this; his first brief tenure as editor of the *Pakistan Times* was filled with storm and ire. I never learned to like the building in Lahore which housed that enormous paper: it clattered so, with people constantly rushing up and down its hallways, ink-damp galleys in their hands. We were to see enough of it, nonetheless, in the next twenty years, during which Pip by turns edited the paper and then was ousted; reappointed, and ousted again. For though the governments and information secretaries did not like him much, Pip's name—like his presence—had a weight, and they had to admit he was competent. I sometimes wished that he were less competent, ready to become instead a sager, quieter soul: but how could that happen when history, dressed as the

*Pakistan Times*, was waiting for him, beckoning him into the longest romance of his life?

Odd, to think that just one man could keep us all so busy. There we were, attendant on his tempestuous career, waiting like proofreaders to go through the galleys of his days, breathless with surprise. He certainly surprised us during the 1965 war, when he offered his services to the government and headed the military public relations service as a colonel in the Pakistan army. He had wonderful stories of those days, of course, of his struggles with his uniform, of how he would zoom up and down the border in a little helicopter, landing next to indifferent farming folk and shouting out, "Where's the war?" We knew he could not last in that environment long and expected him to be out again, founding another paper or returning to the *Pakistan Times*. Those were heady days in Pakistan, with Ayub's empire beginning to crumble and the horizon brightening at the prospect of an alternative, a man called Zulfikar Ali Bhutto. For a while Bhutto and Pip were the closest of friends, but something in their forms of power clashed, making them mistrust each other's version of history. "Ah, Suleri, Suleri," sighed Bhutto when they met, "now all we have left in common are our initials." Papa laughed, because then he was very fond of him, but that was soon to change.

How different Pakistan would be today if Ayub had held elections at that time, in 1968, instead of holding on until the end and then handing power over to—of all people!— Yahya. But military governments, although utterly efficient at starting to rule, do not usually know how to stop—except, of course, General Yahya's government, which held an election and, not knowing how to face its consequences, clamped a massive military emergency on a single province that lead not just to its secession but to the bloody war of Bangladesh. If Ayub had held elections there might still have been a deathly power struggle between Bhutto and Mujib: Mujib, the elected leader of East Pakistan; Bhutto, of West Pakistan. There probably would have been a Bangladesh anyway, but maybe with less blood. Back at the *Pakistan Times*, Pip watched events like a man possessed: he wrote night and day and would not believe it when, during the 1970 election, his workers went out on strike. "The nation is going through a crisis, and you think of a raise?" he thundered to the union representatives. "Is that the yardstick of your devotion?" Apparently it was not, since the strike was soon called off.

With the country absorbing every moment of his attention, Papa thought it was highly unreasonable of his children to distract him from his proper duty by behaving as though they had lives. When Nuz got married, Papa would not speak to her for years. It was all because Baji understandably did not want him to attend the wedding—a small courtesy, you would think, but sufficient to put Pip into a major miff. At the time I did not realize that I was witnessing the formation of a pattern, but—it turns out—after each of his daughter's weddings something in Pip's soul maintains a shuddering silence at the thought of them until, finally, he manages to look up, a mighty resignation in his eyes. The second crisis— an enormous one—came when Ifat decided to marry a polo-playing army man: "But what does he know," Papa asked in horror, "about the genesis of Pakistan?" He still believed he had a veto power over his children's lives, but Ifat was hardly a woman to veto, even when she was six. After Ifat went and married the man, Pip would not let her name be mentioned in his presence, so total was her banishment. They came to an uneasy reconciliation some two years later, but for a while we missed her sorely, hungry for her presence in our lives.

By the time Ifat was allowed to visit us again, my mother's sympathy had trained me to be the second person in the home to decipher my father's impossible hand. It cut out a new task for my afternoons, when I would sit with a Men and Matters article next to me, transcribing into a florid copperplate Papa's ferocious language. His typists and typesetters could read only curly handwriting, so I forced my *g*'s to curl. "The Jamaat-i-Islami opposed the Pakistan movement tooth and nail," I copied out, "it was only after partition that the party changed its colors and Maudoodi reared his ugly head." "Are you sure that isn't libel, Pip?" I asked him doubtfully. Or Mamma and I would look at each other in dismay when Papa called us from his office to command, "Mairi, Sara, about two years ago I wrote an article called 'Whither Basic Democracy?' Find it for me, please." So we would turn to those great sheaves of paper, impossible to file, to hunt and hunt through that familiar discourse for the words of his desire. I did not like to have to handle so much newspaper and sometimes felt as though my fingerprints were wearing out with the impact of all that ink.

But something of our spirits broke, in the war of 1971. It was not so much the country's severing that hurt as the terrible afterimages we had to face: censorship lifted for a flash, flooding us with photographs and stories from the foreign press of what the army actually did in Bangladesh during the months of emergency that preceded the war. "I am not talking about the two-nation theory," I wept to my father, "I am talking about blood!" He would not reply, and so we went our separate ways, he mourning for the mutilation of a theory, and I—more literal—for a limb, or a child, or a voice. Bhutto came to power after the war in Bangladesh, making Pip say darkly, "If he had negotiated, if he had conceded, this would not have happened." Even Bhutto had lost some of the jauntiness that had so won the heart of the electorate of West Pakistan: "Yes, I drink!" he had told his entranced Muslim audience, "But I also work, don't I?" Or in the midst of a formal reception he would choose to join the performers on the stage, to dance and sing with them, "Hé jamalo, ho jamalo!" Our days were more bitter, though, when Bhutto inaugurated his autocratic rule: Papa left the *Pakistan Times*, becoming the government's most vocal critic.

Now we were in trying times. Ifat's hustand was a prisoner of war, putting clouds about her face, clearing only in moments when we talked and watched her two children play. Papa took to praying, which he had never done before; one day I looked up to notice a graying in his eyes and realized in sharp premonition, "Why, Pip is growing blind." History was turning his eyes inward, and even though it was an operable, curable disease, for years we had to wince at the sudden hesitance in his bold stride. "Honestly, Mamma," I couldn't help but grumble, "you'd think he could have chosen a less Miltonic ailment." "Honestly, Sara!" she said in reply.

But we were coming to a parting, Pakistan and I. I felt supped full of history, hungry for flavors less stringent on my palate, less demanding of my loyalty. Ifat told me that she always knew I had to go, "But I don't want to be in the same room when you tell Pip!" she added ruefully. I did not much want to be there myself, did not want to see how scandalized his face would be at the thought that I could thus rob myself of the abundance of his company. It cost me a curious sum of courage when I sat with him through that conversation. For a while he looked at me as though I were telling him that I was not a nation any more, that I was a minority: then, slowly, his face crossed over into dignity. "If I say no, you still will go," he told me quietly. "Go, child. I have no choice."

My mother helped me pack my books; Tillat and Ifat chose my clothes; Irfani found a piece of wood and carved an ashtray for me. Even Allah Ditta the cook stopped grumbling on the morning that I left, saying to me almost fondly, "Who will give me the daily order now?" "Keep on living," Dadi said and barely kissed my head. "The thing that makes me happiest," Mamma wrote to me shortly after, "is the thought of your life." For they were glad to have me gone into some other difference, a world of fewer deadlines, less notoriety. I in the American Midwest woke up to find myself inhabiting an unreal little town that looked to me like toy-land: my hours of rest were happy truants then, filling me with glee. I woke in the morning without a paper at my door and blessed the peace that put me out of it, the endless circulation of news. My life told me that it had long been waiting for this weekend when it could stay in bed: so stay put, then, life, I said, and brought it breakfast too. Of course I also missed my duties, though I would not admit it, and gradually noticed that I did take an interest in the fate of Bhutto's empire: to read that there was rioting in Lahore suddenly made me shiver, to think I was not there. Still, I was happy for a year, even when I caught myself peering around for information in the manner of Pip's Miltonic eyes.

Poor Ifat, she had so many duties in those days, tending to Papa during his two eye operations and then to Mamma in the wicked March she died! Mamma was crossing the road from the university where she taught over to Tollington Market when a rickshaw driver came to knock her down and bruise her from her mind. In the days she teetered on her own brink, she came to consciousness once: she smiled at Ifat, saying strangely, "Send the car for the children, Zia." When I met Ifat later that summer, she solemnly told me all her tales: "When I saw the doctor pump upon her heart—it's the kind of thing you see on television—I knew it was the end." "Oh, Ifat," I mourned to her, "god help us for the way that information comes!" Papa of course was prostrate, broken. I saw fear in him then, for the first time ever, as though my mother's absence made him immediately more parochial, uncertain that the present was a place he could again inhabit. I watched his face struggle with its grief, and felt a deep compassion when I saw how unerringly his mind led him to its only trick of solace, for Papa was not trying to understand how quickly grief becomes its own memorial: he was fighting it instead, and trying to forget.

By that time, Bhutto had been deposed and Zulu Haq was in power. Papa returned to the *Pakistan Times*, and I think that last stint of editing gave him great relief, filling his days again with the great reality of newsprint. But 1979 was a strange year in many ways, for first of all our Dadi died, and then they did in Bhutto. When Zulu Haq took over and Bhutto was imprisoned, I had imagined that he would end like those others—Yahya and Ayub—living out his days under house arrest. It disquieted me, then, when he was put on

trial for murder in a case that seemed inexorably bound to
stop before the thought of clemency, since we already knew
the verdict. Laws were changing in Pakistan, and I had a
dread that the country was prepared to consume the last
vestiges of its compassion. Away in America, I cringed to
hear the unseemly news that Bhutto had been hanged. What
had happened to the memory of those minds, I thought, that
they could so abuse a body that they once had loved? I could
feel that a brute energy was building up in Pakistan, as
though the ghost of that populace—mercilessly cast about in
1947, then again in 1971—had summoned up its strength
again, but this time for revenge. On us, at least, the ven-
geance came.

Ifat died precisely a day after the second anniversary of
my mother's death. She was walking with her husband outside her home in Lahore when a car drove up and knocked
her down and then vanished without a trace. By the time I
got back to Pakistan, it was as though I did not have even the
idea of a sister any more, for Ifat had become the news. Her
name was everywhere, a public domain, blotting out her face
and its finesse into the terrible texture of newsprint. The
mourners who came visiting us seemed quickened with hungry curiosity: I stood by speechless as I watched the world
sensationalize her life, her death. And then came the murder
case, endless investigations that led nowhere but to greater
trouble to our souls. It was Papa's enemies, they said. No, it
was the family, they said. I sat with Tillat and Shahid and Pip
in silence, our hearts afflicted. Our minds were not relieved
to know that Ifat had written me a letter the day before she
died: oh, it felt grotesquely clumsy, waiting for that letter to
be forwarded from America, to see what Ifat said! Her words
to me were sweet, and they spoke about her life, so that—for
me—their reading was almost a reprieve, suggesting endless
possibility of conversation still in store for us. "Be rational,
Sara!" Shahid whispered to me. "That's not a letter to you
now—it's evidence," he said. Ifat's letter, evidence? I said a

quick good-bye to the sweet assurance of those days when I could claim to know the name of things. At that moment, privacy left our lexicon: it surely left my life.

Evidence or not, the letter did not help, and slowly we came to admit to ourselves that our nightmare of detection would not have an end, leaving us always ignorant of its most vital information. Pakistan was very ready to forget: the news had been sensational, but now its day was done. At home, however, we moved round in slow despair, our practice of habit broken. There was no behavior in my mind that did not require painstaking reformulation: how do I lift this glass, I'd think, and take it to my lips? Our only solace was to tend to Ifat's children, three of them now: the youngest, Ayesha, turned six. But Pip was a person deranging through those days, working in a rage to reconstruct the semblance of a thought, and in a forgetful trick I could not understand that he made a separation in his head between himself and Ifat's children. "They belong to their father," he told us angrily, "you cannot interfere." I was amazed to think that he, who had seen families swallowed up before, could expect us also to construct this roughest judgement. "When you go back to America, there's hardly much that you'll do for the children," Shahid told me, "maybe Papa's right." But Shahid, my mind whispered, you just were not here. These mites were not fragments in your hands when they were hours old: you have not felt the funniness with which they grow and grow. You ask me to repudiate, now she is freshly dead, the thing of Ifat's life? But he could not respond to what I did not say. And so my silence hissed to me: stay, in the face of history, harbor to those three most deserving of a cove, since they have lost delicious wind that gave them their desire—or go, but know that you leave with a body derogate, unfit in such desertion to conceive even the idea of a child! Back and forth I went, bandying between the proper duty of my grief: to whom did I owe my allegiance, those who were grieving or the object of that grief? My mind fatigued itself in the anguish of that shilly-shally. And then, I did not stay.

I returned to America conscious of my vanity, the gay pretense with which I had believed that I could take a respite from my life. It was only then that I became historical, a creature gravely ready to admit that significance did not sit upon someone else's table like a magazine to which one could or could not subscribe. I listened to the chattering of my ghosts and told them, "Soft you, I have done the state some service, and you know it." Then I waited for the chastisement I knew I deserved: "You were the state, and yet you did not know!" Oh my mind's fool, I thought, astonished: it has taken you the deaths of a dear mother and a dear sister, the loss of three dear children, before you could contemplate such a dangerous simplicity? You were born fit; you rendered yourself unfit. Now comes the time when you must make yourself historical.

An impossible act, however, to explain to Pip, who needed badly to retain his version as the only form of history. Pip was very gentle when we next met, in Williamstown, where I had packed away my life of lazy Sundays and now begun to work. He would not look on me as on a renegade, sending instead old stories circulating between us, familiars that I was glad to have for company. Of course he was going to write his memoirs, he announced, and call it *Boys Will Be Boys*: he knew how that title made me laugh. We talked of politics rather than of my return, while the names of our dead hung about us like the atmosphere in which we breathed and spoke. I trounced the Islamization of Pakistan to him; he trounced it back to me. "The genesis of Pakistan was not Islam!" he shouted, as I knew he would, "It was different—it was Muslim nationhood!" All the while I knew he still believed that it was possible for me to go back and to live with him, reluctant as he was to read the "never" in my eyes. "Do you ever have sensations of daughterly compunction?" he asked me, touchingly. "Sometimes, Papa," I breathed, "I do." Then he took pity on me, and brightened up his tone to tell me once again his favorite story of my babyhood. He had returned from Europe late in the night and on a warm Karachi morning was happy to be sitting in his room again, kissing us one by one as we got up. I was the last to awake and came bustling into his bedroom with great welcome, announcing myself as I ran in, "Another girl!" I could never quite see why that story had such meaning for him, but to Pip it defined my life. "Anther girl, anther girl!" he repeated to me in Williamstown, bright laughter on his face.

Did he have an inkling then, when Pip went back to Pakistan alone, a dreadful thought to him? He had his paper still, to preoccupy both night and day with deadline's sweet familiarity, but history was not sufficient then to keep the demons from his soul. Burying my mother had been bad enough, but burying Ifat in the gravespace where he hoped to lie was terrifying, making his bed each night a place where he must work to bury her again. I mourned to imagine the extremity of that labor, wondering when it would compel him to forgetfulness, his old luxurious habit. What I did not know was that this work was also making Papa feel the need to be historical: one day he gave a mighty sob, arose, and glanced around Lahore. Then he found himself another daughter. It was a contingency that had not occurred to me, until I got Nuzzi's letter. I was glad that I heard it from her and that her unpunctuation made me see the humor of this astounding information: "Irfani is the Sherlock Holmes in this," Nuzzi scrawled, "But it has been in the papers too so Sara you must know that Papa's adopted a daughter and we have a new sister now." "Anther girl, indeed!" I exclaimed. "I asked him why he hadn't remarried because I thought he had enough daughters already but he did not really reply." "Ah, Papa," I thought, "you have laughed tears to my eyes, for even if you had worked on it for years—albeit un-knowingly—you could not have hit upon a more adequate revenge!" I shook my head throughout the day, until that evening Shahid called: "You've heard what's happened, I suppose." I told him that although I'd always known that Pip was brilliant at fresh starts, such a bigning was big enough to take my breath away. "In terms of the limit, it is quite Pip-pish," was all that Shahid had left to say. We shook our heads in unison over the phone at this preponderance of reality. "And then the name," he added, "the strangeness of the name." "What is the name?" I asked him, interested. Shahid gave a transatlantic shiver. "She's called Shahida!" he said.

Thus it happened that I was distracted once again—long after I thought I had outlived such moments of interruption—to ponder in slow thought the amazement of that man. With professional efficiency, as though orchestrating governmental change, Pip cleared the family stage of his mind and ushered a new one in. It made me admit that I would never be immune to the exigencies of information: in Pakistan, the propriety of every eyebrow raised itself at Pip, whose publicity insisted that this was his play, both to direct and to act in. What could we do, we asked one another, but applaud, as though we were applauding the tragic failure of farce? Historical myself, it made me recognize the soil that Pip was asserting when, on my next visit to Pakistan, I found him in the Punjabi pink, his brand-new daughter by his side. Weeping for my dead was quite another issue: his demeanor made me look at him quizzically, and he look at me gruffly, so that for the first time in years the airspace between us was rife with comedy again. "I have my needs," he snarled when we were once alone. "You do, indeed," I answered seriously. Then his face fell away from its defense into a quick crossing of dignity: "It was just a matter of shamelessness and fatigue, simply that," he sighed.

Now Papa has left the *Pakistan Times*, and hates it, his retirement. It leaves him lying in a bed surrounded by telephones that will not ring, and he hates such active suspension. There is nothing of my mother left in his house now, of course, and our visits seem to cause him increasing unease, reminding him of some other thing that he once knew, a memory international. He still has Shahida, but "I am alone, alone!" he groaned to me when I last went to see him in Islamabad. I pointed out to him that in the last fifty years he had had two wives, six children, eleven grandchildren, and now also had a brand-new daughter. "And that's only your official record!" I added, jauntily. But Pip did not want to leave his mood of darkening cloud. "I have done nothing with my life!" he cried, "I have written nothing!" I told him that he had all the time to make a bigning now and write *Boys Will Be Boys*—a wonderful book, I knew. He shook his mane and sighed, gazing down upon his vacant fingers. "What would I say," he wondered to himself instead of me, "and what could I just not?" Then, "For, Sara, I have done some terrible things!" "Such as, Papa?" I asked gently, sad at this confession, coming latter-day. I was relieved when he became professional again about the business of his news. "If God has been merciful enough to keep my secrets," retorted Pip, "should I be so ungrateful as to tell them to you?" No, my dear, my dear, I thought to myself, protect my being in the end and keep some information from me. That night I knew I should not visit him again if I wished to spare his soul chagrin, and so I practiced at its utterance, good-bye, and then good-bye.

Years ago, shortly after Mamma died, Tillat and I both noticed and wondered at Papa's latest nervous quirk. He had begun to use his index finger as a pen, making it in constant scribbles write on each surface it could find. He did not seem aware of this new habit, but whether he was eating at the table or ensconced in his old green chair, Papa's finger moved on in ghostly hieroglyphics, as though to abjure the idiosyncrasy of speech. "But what is he writing?" Tillat marveled. "It must be something Urdu, for he's moving from right to left." I told her I was sure that she had misread the event, that his finger moved with the pattern of the fabric, left to right. "Are you certain?" she answered, disbelievingly, "I could swear that it looked like Urdu." But as we whispered on in the half-light, we both felt cognizant of a more pressing issue: in a room we could not see, a hand was still awake. It sought the secrecy of surface in the dark, and its finger was writing, writing.

# THE IMMODERATION
# OF IFAT

At first I thought she was the air I breathed, but Ifat was prior, prior. Before my mechanical bellows hit the air to take up their fanning habit, Ifat had preceded me, leaving her haunting aura in all my mother's secret crevices: in the most constructive period of my life she lay around me like an umbilical fluid, yellow and persistent. I was asleep inside her influence when I did not yet know how to sleep. In later years such envelopment would lend a curiosity to my regard, which was uncertain whether an inward musing would not suffice—since there was so much of her inside me—in place of what it meant to look at her. But how could I abstain from looking? For if Shahid was the apple of my eye when I was six, Ifat belonged to a more burnished complexion and was the golden apples of my soul.

Was she twin, or is that merely my imagination? Could it be possible that one egg in its efficient subdivisions became forgetful for a while—my company of cells went wandering off bemused and was not missed—until four years later they remembered to be born, the sleepy side of Ifat? It cannot be, for she was twinned before my time, her face already raising to the power of some other number, which danced about her shoulder like a spirit minuscule. And she needed no lessons from me about how to conduct her always instantaneous sleep! Sleep would come and hold her like a membrane does, until her voice at night was the only one I've heard to tell me quite so clearly, "There are two chords of voice inside my throat." Once it was day again, how I could listen to those humming things, which cajoled each other, danced and ran, in the manner that her face ran, too, weaving in and out of the eddies of her voice. They worked in unison at a display brilliant and precise as water, when water wishes to perform both in and out of light. So of course I was not needed to make Ifat two: before I had even dreamed of number, she had enacted out a multitude. There always were, for instance, several voices in her single throat.

I thought of it, the trick of Ifat's speech and the colloquy that it conducted with her face, when my friend Jonathan was kindly driving me through New Haven's unloveliness. He was driving me home—a kind thing to do—and it set him brooding on all the other ways he could be kind to me. "It's all very well, you know," he murmured, "to be obsessional." We were driving down a one-way street. "But why do it so thoroughly, arrest yourself in a prosopopoeic posture that retards you from your real work?" I looked out the window at people shoveling hateful snow. "Maybe this is my work," I suggested finally. Jonathan's hands left the wheel in a moment of abbreviated exasperation, but then he softened, liberal toward me. "Alright. So now you have to write about your sister's death." "Nonsense!" I replied indignantly, and then the subject changed, as we reached home. But later on I wondered at that conversation, and the scandal in my voice when I cried out, "Nonsense!" What did it mean, I wondered. Then I realized what I must have known all along: of course, Ifat's story has nothing to do with dying; it has to do with the price a mind must pay when it lives in a beautiful body.

Of all her haunting aspects that return to me, I often am most pleased when I recollect her wrist. Ifat imposed an order on her bones that gave her gestures of an unsuspected strength: her wrists were such a vessel. There was no jar, no bottle in the house which could resist that flick of wrist, and in arm wrestling once she dropped Shahid down, to cries of everyone's amazement. We liked to watch her wield her slender tools with such efficient hygiene, so "Let Ifat open the olives," we'd agree, and when of course she did in one clean twist, our admiration exceeded olives. She was the nutty bone our teeth would hit when we wished to take upon our tongue that collusion of taste and texture. Ifat was always two. In moments when her affection felt most fierce to her, she would send out two fingers to bracelet tightly the wrist of whoever was beside her and gave her joy: when that wrist was mine, I had no way of uttering the honor to my radius and ulna. In later years, particularly, Ifat would suddenly and wordlessly grasp my wrist, making my hand, like a dying moth or a creature not knowing what to do with suffocation, flutter out, "Don't let go; don't let go."

"Don't let go, Ifat!" I screamed out in alarm when she veered me back and forth on the world's most perfect swing. There is a chinar tree in Nathia Gali growing upon a silent verge: some large-spirited person has hung a swing from its most massive limb so that the seat swings out to hurtle a body over that chasmic valley, whose terraced rice fields gleam, green and tiny, thousands of feet below. That swing was one of Ifat's passions as a child, and once she had had her manic fill of movement, she would test my mettle by pushing me back and forth over that heart's leap of a fall. I did not know which I liked better: the ecstasy of space such motion gave me or the approval in Ifat's eye when—after I had collapsed trembling on the hill—she'd say, "That was brave of you, Sara, since you are so small!" She was always fair about making concessions to my size: even when I annoyed her, she would glance at me gloomily and say, "I suppose you can't help it, since you are so small." Of course I fought against such diminution, forcing my mind into a trot to keep up with her and the swiftness of her thought. "Shahid is also smaller than you," I reminded her once when she seemed to be slipping beyond my grasp. "That's different, he's a boy." But when I sought to question her on why my girlhood mattered to my size, she had passed away from listening: "Sara," she said firmly, "I can't explain what you're too young to see."

What I could see, however—even then, when she was eight—was the lasting glamour of a face that both did and did not know the nature of its impact. For her beauty's commonplace was not aware of what transpired on her face when feature fell in with spirit. It was my first experience of aesthetic joy to watch her expression spilling over with laughter, or amazement, or whatever else was prompting her to feel alive at a given moment of the day. To such a sight my father responded with a bright delight, looking at her only with open admiration, but I sometimes noticed that my mother would seem saddened to be a witness of that gay excess. It was as though Ifat's grace was frightening to her, as she watched her child and had to contemplate what the world could exact from grace. How I must concentrate, she thought, in order to protect this girl from what could be the portion of such extravagance of face. It made her soul subdued and move in measure when she saw the sudden theater of Ifat's eyes: a theater unable to envisage a curtain or the quick falling of a duskless night. So Mamma gravely curtained Ifat then, adopting a twilight tone that seemed to say, bright daylight of my daughter, look at me and learn. But Ifat was too interested in adoration to consider what else my mother's manner could suggest: "Oh softness of my mother!" she'd exclaim. Thus lesson only gave occasion to what it sought to hide. "What gave you such green eyes, what gave you such softness?" Ifat adored.

Could that be it, an unwitting absorption of my mother's fear, that causes all those sharp angles to accrue around my earliest images of Ifat? I am crying along a roadside in Karachi that is a stony and resistant surface on which to run and cry, but she has left me far behind, so I know that I will never catch up with her and that I no longer want to be the only audience to my tears. Then, shortly after I am three years old, sitting on the deep veranda of a Karachi house, watching in admiration as Ifat twirls her weight upon a heavy rope that holds thick bamboo screens in place, now rolled stiffly up to let in the tepid evening breeze. Ifat dances, twirls and whirls—her white muslin frock is a further admiration round her limbs—until her forehead meets with sickening crack an evil abutment of plaster. How efficiently the fabric of her dress absorbs the abundance of her blood! I hear Ifat screaming "Papa, Papa!" shaking off her entanglement in rope and the sharpness of her fall and the little wounded sounds that Shahid and I keep darting round her. As Papa runs out from his study, Ifat is able to command, almost with impatience, "Now hold me while I die."

She didn't, of course, and her seven-year-old cranium was knitting before the three of us had really satisfied our taste for the glory of her wound. But Ifat still lay in her blue bed and behaved as though nothing could be averted now. It was as though her mastery over us had been extended beyond the weight of years—three over Shahid, four over me—to address us henceforth with the infinite knowledge of the grave. So it did not matter that two days later not even that cumbersome gauze bandage, an ill-tied turban on her head, could keep Ifat in her bed. Even when she was soon up again and playing, she still had that bloodletting over us, making her absolute and awesome to our eyes.

Some two decades later Ifat described her fall to me as though I had not been there, and it was entrancing to witness that event again from, as it were, the opposite angle of the room. She did not pay particular attention to the hurt itself nor to the imperious evocations of death that it unleashed in her. Instead, she told me about what it was like at night to wait for the moistness of that wound to heal and then to run a finger through her hair, feeling the increasingly stiff joy of that dry extraneous growth, with which she could tamper, if she chose. For Ifat, the event clinched her perception of bodily secrecy and the illicit texture of what happens when something is added onto or subtracted from flesh. For me, however, it was and still remains my sharpest consciousness of the publicity of blood.

Keen red blood, coursing down her leopard's skull! The image made me shudder many years afterward when we were merely playing and something in her imperiousness reminded of how she could hurt. For games were Ifat's provenance: she made us play and play until the very intensity of her invention made us feel as though we collaborated with her in the most significant work of our lives. When I woke in the morning, I would slowly think, I wonder what we will play today, and before I was properly awake, Ifat would be upon me, shaking me to action: "You're Belinda and Shahid's Pepito and I'm Diana"; "You're Gray Rabbit and Shahid is Mole and I'm the Crab"; "Today we're going to play at Holmes." Holmes was an elaborate invention through which Ifat made our toys familial to us: each one had its proper station of relationship, and new toys in the fold had to undergo a stringent initiation before they were admitted to that private world. A woollen animal knitted expressly for Shahid (What was Goodboy's sweet face meant to signify? A dog? Perhaps a bear?) was the bad-boy stranger in our games for months until Ifat declared, "He's home—he can be a good boy now." And so we solemnly welcomed him into our midst and named him Goodboy: Goodboy soon became so much a part of us that he even married the Princess of Loveliness—Ifat's favorite doll—after we had determined that he was her long-lost brother, most deserving to have her as his wife. They were intricately brothered and sistered, all our toys, as we made them wed and interwed.

" 'Who Killed Cock Robin?'—what a strange song it is, Ifat," I said to her one day. " 'I, said the sparrow, with my bow and arrow'—how odd that he should confess it straightaway!" "You know what he's confessing, don't you?" replied Ifat with a meaningful look that always made me feel most ignorant. "It's all about sex!" And then, rising to the horror on my face, she added, "Of course you know that's what nursery rhymes are all about!" Ifat looked pleased at this. "You know, don't you, that all those rhymes are just a way of telling children about the horrid parts of sex?" I at eight did not want to know, feeling squeamish at the relentlessness of her claim. "Don't tell me, Ifat, don't," I begged, until her satisfaction was nearly brimming over. "What!" she exclaimed cheerfully, " 'Put on the pan, says greedy Nan, / Let's sup before we go'? 'She cut off their tails with a carving knife / Did you ever see such a sight in your life'?—Come on, Sara, see what you must see!" I crumpled, seeing it, for Ifat's devastating knowledge seemed designed to rob me of the pale of innocence, insisting that innocence was a lie, a most pallid place to be! "Don't you think that there are some things you shouldn't tell me?" I asked her once, gloomily, after she had filled my evening with hair-raising representations of bodily functions. "Don't you think it may be bad for me?" "If you let it fester, that's your fault," Ifat answered in reproof. "Tomorrow I'll tell you why Jack Sprat could eat no fat and his wife could eat no lean!" And then, leaving me to contemplate her dreadful promise, she turned round and went to sleep.

What else could she be coupled with when she had her discourse by her? She presented herself to the world as a pair in the whitest days of her girlhood, so that looking and listening leaked their knowledge into one another in a magic of multiplication. Her talk was like a creature next to her, a golden retriever of Ifat's singular expression or, better still, a lion padding in startling fashion about the house. Years later, when Richard X. swept into my home with his dog Lulu by his side, something of his buoyancy made me tell him cautiously, "You can remind me slightly of my sister." I intended it to be the highest compliment that I could pay, not realizing at the time that to a man so conscious of the peculiarities of manhood such an analogy could only perplex. "Did you like her?" asked Richard in the wistful way he had of always saying in secret, "Please like me." "Like her?—Oh yes," I said quietly, "yes, I did like Ifat." But naming her put the unpronounceability of my life between us in a way that gave him unease: he did not wish to see me framed by family just then but to picture me alone instead and isolate me in his gaze.

"If anyone hurts you, Sara," Ifat said to me on the day I turned nineteen, "make sure you tell me who it is, so that I can kill them, slowly." For a moment she looked mournful with protection but then, at the execution of revenge, quite pleased. "I'll do a Dadi, chop up their livers into little bits and feed them to the crows," she added, echoing my Dadi's favorite curse. We had just driven to Gulberg Market in Lahore, and as she sat waiting for me in the car, she saw two vagabonds drive up to graze me slightly when I crossed the road. I think they only wished to startle me, wanting for some reason to see a woman look afraid, but swiftly came their punishment. Ifat drove fiercely after them, forced their car off the road, and then used her car as a battering ram, causing considerable damage to both vehicles. "Are you mad?" said the vagabonds, aghast. "How dare you touch my sister?" Ifat hissed. By then quite a crowd had gathered, in the habit of Lahore's instant assembly of spectatorship, so Ifat was surrounded with supporters cheering on her bravery. "Don't you have any sisters yourselves, you louts?" they told the astounded vagabonds. "Don't you understand what it is to protect the honor of your sister?" The vagabonds drove off without a word, dented and dumbfounded. "You've lost a headlight," I told Ifat as I got back into the car, noticing her knuckles white with rage. "If anyone hurts a hair of your head, Sara," Ifat told me as we drove home, "I will not let them live." Her voice seemed overburdened with knowledge at that moment: it made me stare down at the birthday cake sitting on my lap and think, "Dear god, don't let her hurt."

I had already watched her accrue the tragedy of adolescence, days she endured only in the deepest mourning. Even then there was an energy to her manner that belied her tone: "Oh, I am Wednesday's child!" she would exclaim.

"Wednesday's, full of woe!" In that era she hated her body, which had become beautiful in a way that was too womanly for her tastes, hungry for childhood's swifter grace. So Ifat would hold her face fastidiously, a walking crown above such bodily disdain, as though she would concede to walking beside her body but would not inhabit it, not yet. "Look at the hair on my arms!" she said to me with horror. "It's too horrible—I'd need a forest fire to get rid of all this growth on my limbs!" She was by no means ready to accept the modifications in her own aesthetic that existence was imposing on her and disavowed its strictures, even when they gave her great increments of grace. Thus Ifat left her body sitting by the fire and sauntered off to stare out the window in the opposite direction, for there were always several Ifats with us in a room. Hinged to her like a hotel door, what could I do but keep ushering them in, those successions of her face?

But she had reason to be burdened. Both my parents looked at her with such keen eyes that it must have been a strain on her good humor—she was a most good-humored girl—to sustain the pressure of that gaze. My mother was always cautious, maintaining her exemplary trick of perpetual understatement in order to teach Ifat something of the art of moderation. She developed habits that Ifat passionately admired but could not emulate, for Ifat's habits were my father's. From him she learned her stance of wild inquiry, the arrogant angle at which she held her head. It was her gesture of devotion to him, really, the proud position she maintained when—to the complete devastation of domestic serenity—those two wills clashed. It made me groan aloud to think that Papa could not see that Ifat was simply loving him for what he was when she handed back to him, gesture by gesture, his prickling independence of style. But he could not see deeply enough into the lonely work of this fidelity, noticing only with alarm her flaring spirit, so much like his own. "When Ifat learns to love another man, what will happen to it, her habit of fidelity?" I could read written in my mother's eyes.

And so there was an even greater tentativeness to Mamma's touch when she sat down at her piano to play a while and then to softly sing,

> Oh sisters two, how may we do,
> for to preserve this day?
> This poor youngling, for whom we sing,
> Bye bye, lully, lullay.

I felt it sharply, when Ifat learned to love another man. There were always in her great reserves of devotion to dispense: I did not feel deprived but feared that it would be too expensive to her spirit to utter to my father such a complete good-bye. After having lived for years with his endless eloquence of voice, how could she do it, choose to love a silent man? So I warned her against Javed and the ways he could be alien: "He sees your face," I warned, "and not the spirit that constructs your face." Ifat would not listen. It put a gulf between us in those years before she ran away from home and married him, because my disapproval hurt, making her instinctively hide in order to protect her love. "If anything needs that much protection," I told her, "you know it must be wrong." Then I hated myself for being right, when I saw the quick cloud of pain that I had cast about her eyes. So those years in Lahore were difficult with my disapproval, although even I had to laugh on the night when Javed, prowling round the house in amorous pursuit of Ifat, lay down on Dadi's bed. He was waiting for Ifat in the garden and saw what he thought was an empty bed, only to discover that the tiny curlicue of my Dadi was lying next to him, asleep beneath the stars. What did he signify to her? For a while I was perplexed, until I slowly saw that rather than at a man, I should be looking at the way Javed signified to Ifat a complete immersion into Pakistan. She was living here for good now, she must have thought, so why not do it well? And what greater gift could she give my father than literally to become the land he had helped to make? He, of course, could never see the touching loyalty of this decision, but then our adulthood would often seem to him betrayal's synonym. He could not countenance her love for a polo-playing army man, a spark about the town, not stopping to consider that Ifat was his child and well designed to match adamant with adamant, iron with iron. Javed's elder brother was in prison at that time—for rape, after a trial of great notoriety—but the more prudence that amassed against him, the more resolution to Ifat's loyalty. "Oh, girl," I groaned to myself in exasperation, "why are you so perishably pretty? Who put such pretty notions in your head?" By this time Ifat was in college at Kinnaird, willing a greater distance between my father and herself in a determination uncannily like his in tone. And then, with perverse aplomb, she chose to enter into the heart of Pakistan in the most un-Pakistani way possible: she ran away from Kinnaird and called home a few days later to say, bravely, "Papa, I'm married." "Congratulations," he replied, put down the phone, and refused to utter her name again for years. Ifat was then nineteen.

Adrift from each familiar she had known, what energies my sister devoted to Pakistan! First she learned how to speak Punjabi and then graduated to the Jehlum dialect, spoken in the region from which Javed's family came. She taught herself the names and stations of a hundred-odd relations, intuiting how each of them would wish to be addressed. She learned more than I will ever know about the history of the army, and then she turned to polo's ins and outs. The game, she discovered, had originated in the valleys of Kaghan where, in place of a ball, the tribes most commonly played with an enemy's head instead: "Oh," said Ifat, digested it, and moved on to something else. She went with her mother-in-law to the family's ancestral village in the Punjab to perform an annual sacrifice of some poor animal—a goat was killed for god and then doled out to the village's poor. Later she discovered that the rite was a traditional atonement, performed on the spot where Javed's great-grandfather had slain his infant daughter, so aggrieved was he to have a female as a child. "Oh!" said Ifat and listened, white as ice. She listened to her father-in-law, the brigadier, a polo-playing man, tell her that he wanted his four sons to be gentlemen, he did not want them to be cads. She listened to all this, and then she taught herself the most significant task of them all. She learned the names of Pakistan.

For never has there been, in modern times, such a Homeric world, where so much value is pinned onto the utterance of name! Entire conversations, entire lives, are devoted to the act of naming people, and in Pakistan the affluent would be totally devoid of talk if they were unable to take names in vain. Caste and all its subclassifications are recreated every day in the structure of a conversation that knows which names to name: "Do you know Puppoo and Lola?" "You mean Bunty's cousins?" "No, Bunty's cousins are Lali and Cheeno, I'm talking about the Shah Nazir family—you know, Dippoo's closest friends." "Oh, of course, I used to meet them all the time at Daisy Aunty's place!" For everyone has a family name and then a diminutive name, so that to learn an ordinary name is not enough—you must also know that Zahid is Podger, and Seema is Nikki, and Rehana is Chunni, and on and on. To each name attaches a tale, and the tales give shape to the day. "Poor Goga, she's so cut up! I think she really misses Chandni quite a lot." "What is the Chandni story, though?" "Darling, all Karachi knows! When Saeed discovered that she was having an affair with Billo, he just couldn't handle it—he had to have her killed!" We had felt too supercilious, in our youth, to bother with this lingo, so it was somewhat of a surprise to hear such names on Ifat's lips. She was permitted to return only after long negotiations: an energetic lady, Aunty Nuri, undertook to mediate between the brigadier and Pip until—under her auspices—a reconciliation of the clans was tautly staged. "I can't stand it," Shahid told me afterward, "when Ifat talks Punjabi or does this Nikki Pikki stuff!" "Well, it must have been hard work," I mused. In any case, I was distracted. For when we met again, how strange I felt to notice that Ifat's beautiful body, which I had missed so much, was now convex with a child.

I wanted to shield her, but I did not have the means. In the pink house on the hill—the brigadier's invention—Ifat was public, praiseworthy for her beauty, while in ours she was treated with a strict formality. My father would never properly forgive her, and my mother's quaintly decorous way sought to extend privacy to Ifat now that she thought her daughter belonged to a different life. So in the end there was no place left where Ifat could return: in each room she was new. "Will no one ever let that girl be at home," I thought, protection spluttering in me like the sulphur smell of a match that flares beyond the call of duty. Ifat watched my face; "It doesn't matter, Sara," she once told me ruefully. "Men live in homes, and women live in bodies." For she was preoccupied with the creature living inside her: I could watch her make a dwelling of her demeanor, a startling place in which to live. My heart was wrenched to see her lying there later, with her infant boy next to her side, red and wrinkled as an infant is after living so long in water! Ifat's eyes smiled at me from her bed, as she lay with her beauty and her discourse and now a baby, too. Your father called you Taimur, child, as in Tamburlaine, a curious appellation for your sweetest disposition, you little infant boy.

What happened, in the war? Javed had been sent to Bangladesh in the era of the emergency. He came back wounded for a month once, and people said that in his impetuous way he had simply shot himself so he could return to look at Ifat's face. "Don't say such things to me, please!" I said. But then the war began, those bitter days for all. The naming games that went on in the drawing rooms of Pakistan now turned their poison outward: it was no longer enough to say, "Do you know Kittoo?"; it was necessary to add, "He died on the Sargodha front," or "Last night Zafar died." I lived with Ifat in the pink house on the hill, sitting with her as those names came tolling in, cold terror in our eyes. During each air raid, the brigadier would stride into the garden, barking out commands to the soldiers who were operating the antiaircraft guns installed on the top of his house: gradually it became a practice of us all to trail into the garden after him, gazing up at those atrocious noises in the sky. The war was brief, but the waiting of those days was long, and it was followed only by a longer waiting when, after the fall of Dacca, we discovered that Javed was alive in India, a prisoner of war. Ifat was pregnant again, but before the daughter that she bore could see her father, the child would be almost two.

Ifat put on her bridal clothes the day Javed returned. What festivity went quickening through our house in Lahore, making us wince to contemplate the gravity of her joy. Fawzi took a photograph of Ifat on that day: it is an uncanny image, which almost seems to know what it must represent, the twinning impulses of Ifat's soul. She stands white and erect, glancing down at a diagonal to the tugging of her daughter Alia's hand. She seems tall and finely boned, head bowed in the face of its own beauty, quite grave to be what it must be. Her slenderness is such as to suggest a keen fragility, most poignant to me, so that when the photograph first met my eyes I cried aloud, "I must protect this girl!"

Those were peculiar days in Pakistan, but the country made quick provisions to forget the war in Bangladesh; when two years later the prisoners of that war finally returned, they came back to a world that did not really want to hear the kind of stories they had to tell. One day, standing in the dining room, Javed suddenly began to describe what he had felt during his first killing. I stopped still, and my head swam at the thought of what came next, overwhelming me with images of what he must have seen. My terror asked me, how will Ifat do it, make Javed's mind a human home again and take those stories from his head? That was the most arduous labor of Ifat's life, as she began with great reserve to bring her husband home again. She matched her courage with compassion, working hard to counteract those three years brutalized, that waste of life. It made me hold my breath to see such concentration on her face, to see her biting her lip—the mannerism of her childhood—trying brick by brick to break that prison down. The only way in which she can do it, I thought to myself, is by first learning what that prison was: what anecdotes must fill her evenings now, what intensity of detail? "If anyone can do it," I told my mother, "Ifat can." "Yes," said Mamma, "she is generous in that way—if anybody can . . . " And then we looked away from one another, silent with dismay.

After Javed left the army, they moved to Sargodha, an uninteresting part of the Punjab, where he took to cultivating land and opening a stud farm. By the next time we met Ifat, she could tell us with fine verve every detail of how that farm was run and how the world breeds polo ponies. I could not help laughing at this incongruous linkage: the finesse of Ifat's thought and the breeding of a horse! Still, she made her stories funny, almost as if she enjoyed it all, never talking about the effort of her secret work. She would saunter into our house, with three children now, along with her discourse and her face, making abundant company. "Thank goodness you look like yourself, Ifat." I hugged my welcome. "I could not bear it if you looked horsey." "Me?" said Ifat, drawing up her scorn, "Do I have yokel's hands?" For we wished only to joke with one another now, telling minor stories, only dainty tales. I felt that I owed her the courtesy of silence on her life's score, as though to be unquestioning in my attention would be the deftest way to demonstrate my sympathy. We developed new patterns of conversation, then, in which phrases floated between us in an unsaid context so limpid that it could dazzle me. It caused her dazzling face the least distress, I hoped, to be surrounded by a discretion so complete as to be dazzling. "Always two," I murmured in her direction, "always two." Ifat smiled a little wearily at that and glanced at me. "They told me I was everything," she sighed, "They lied; I am not beauty-proof."

She walked as erectly as ever, through the fierce reclamation of those times. I wondered about the progress of her work, whether or not her manner of making welcome would suffice: could such a will for healing, by ill luck, serve to magnify the bruise's sense that it was just a shoddy bruise? If that were true, more bruising would come—save her, I begged my limpid context, save her from being bruised. But I would be angry in Lahore when company eager over Javed's name brought me tales of wealth and scandal, waiting for my verdict. "You must not say such things about my sister's husband," I said slowly, "It is impolite." For surely it was discourteous, I felt, for them to bring such tales to me, as though some third person could ever understand the nature of Ifat's work. If only you could remain unnoticed, I told her in my mind, then such indignity would not be cast at the flamboyance of your face. Beauty is a whip they should not use, but will, your trouble being that even the crudest eye that looks at you can believe it comprehends. I winced for Ifat, then. "Brave girl," I said, "ignore the world: continue with your task."

I think it was an irritant to the world, her continued merriment. Nor was this pretense: Ifat was good at getting at joy, as the shape of her eyes would often attest. Some of the most festive moments in my life occurred when Ifat simply walked into my room: she would visit on winter afternoons, sitting upstairs in my red room with Tillat and me, the three of us cross-legged upon the bed. And what exclamation of delight we made when the door quietly opened to my mother's touch, bringing her into our midst with a little smile and a pansy in her hand. "I've just been walking in the garden," she murmured absently, "and I found this pansy . . . " It was often her way of starting conversation, to walk into a room with a flower or pebble, simply saying, "Look . . . " "Oh, Mamma, what a beautiful pansy!" we exclaimed, ravished by her, and handed it around. "Yes, it is rather, isn't it," she said, turning to leave, until, "Don't go, Mamma, don't go! Stay and talk to us," we begged.

Those were the moments that Ifat and I had to collect and recollect after Mamma died. It changed the tenor of our talk again, for then our context had no option but to rise weightless, entranced by her remaining aura. Ifat told me at exquisite pace the stories of her soul: a few months earlier, some sickness had made her flee her family and come to stay at home. She would lie on the sofa, sleeping fitfully throughout the day, while Mamma would be reading student papers at a table close at hand. "And when I woke, she'd smile at me," marveled Ifat, as though recounting miracle. "When I awoke, she'd smile!" "But I was angry at her, Ifat," I confessed, "I felt that someone was handing me a relic of her, some rag doll, and I refused to kiss those button eyes," Ifat shook her lovely head: "Poor Sara, you should have come home then . . . " We were silent for a while. "I miss her," Ifat sighed.

"Although," she added, "a woman can't come home." Her face had clouded, then, making me watch intently the way that meaning shadowed itself, came and went around her eyes. "Why, Ifat?" I finally asked. "Oh, home is where your mother is, one; it is when you are mother, two; and in between it's almost as though your spirit must retract . . ."—she was concentrating now, in the earnest way she concentrated as a child—"your spirit must become a tiny, concentrated little thing, so that your body feels like a spacious place in which to live—is that right, Sara?" she asked me, suddenly tentative. "Perhaps," I said, "perhaps. But when I look at you, Ifat, I am in home's element!" Ifat's two fingers suddenly grasped my wrist. "You know the profit to me, all these years, from your support?" "But Ifat," I said with sudden tears, "to have you as sister is a high honor of my life!" Then we rose and turned to other things, conscious of having uttered all that could be said.

Now it is sweet relief to me to know I need not labor to describe what happened in my mind when Ifat died. I was in surprise. The thickness of event made me a rigid thing, whose thoughts came one by one, as if in pain. I found myself inhabiting a flattened day in which nothing could be two: where is the woman of addition? my mind inquired of me. I could not conceive her body, then, nor tolerate the tales of that body's death, the angle of its face, the bruise upon its neck. What would I not have done, I mused, to keep you from that bruise? But then I felt most vain, most vain. "I did not do enough for your strong heart when doing was open to me," I cried out, "How was I to know we had not years and years? Think of me as the cloth they put around you, some indifferent thing, when you most lithe in all your faith became inflexible!" A curious end for such a moving body, one that, like water, moved most generously in light.

Then commenced keen labor. I was imitating all of them, I knew, my mother's laborious production of her five, my sisters' of their seven (at that stage), so it was their sweat that wet my head, their pushing motion that allowed me to extract, in stifled screams, Ifat from her tales. We picked up our idea of her as though it were an infant, slippery in our hands with birthing fluids, a notion most deserving of warm water. Let us wash the word of murder from her limbs, we said, let us transcribe her into some more seemly idiom. And so with painful labor we placed Ifat's body in a different discourse, words as private and precise as water when water wishes to perform both in and out of light. Let it lie hidden in my eye, I thought, her tiny spirit, buoyant in the excessive salt of that dead sea, so that henceforth too she can direct my gaze, a strange happening, phosphorescent!

Around us, in the city, talk of murder rose like a pestilence, making it a painful act ever to leave the house. My face felt nude, and for the first time in my life I wished I were a woman who could wear a veil, an advertisement of anonymity to mirror all the blankness in my mind. At home I had Shahid and Tillat and Nuz, and we talked and laughed as often as we could, but our hearts were strung with silence. Ifat would like it if we laughed, we knew, and so all of us tried: Shahid rediscovered "Uncle Tom Cobbleigh," his favorite song from childhood, and entertained us for hours with his ingenious adaptations: "Oh, what shall we do with Nuzzi Begum? Pill-popping, pill-popping, pill-popping, pill-popping, and Sara and Farni and all, and Sara and Farni and all." Tillat and I totally disgraced ourselves when one of the mourners who came visiting us, a lady with a hearing aid, warned us that her battery was down and we would have to speak quite loudly. By the third time I had to bellow, "Yes, it is very sad!" to her persistent "What?" Tillat's strength broke down, and we both burst into some of the most uncontrollable laughter that we have ever laughed. Nuz and I noticed that occasionally our visitors would whisper to each other, "That's the half-sister," so we staged some half-sisterly fights for their benefit: I called her short and dark; she called me cold and proud. Then we would take flowers to the cemetery, a companionable thing to do, and when Shahid spread a sheet of roses on the grave, a look of satisfaction crossed his face that I had last seen when I watched him feed his daughter. It brought to mind the most wrenching question of those days: what could we do for Ifat's children?

As the talk of murder settled into irresolution, the rift between my father's house and the brigadier's became complete. Papa insisted that the children belonged with Javed now, that they could only suffer from our influence. "I'm used to thinking more highly of what it means to be loved by me," I answered ruefully. We played with them while we were there, but then they left us for the pink house on the hill, and in our secret minds we all realized that they would, they must, forget. We would not tell one another what we knew, for it seemed the worst disloyalty of all to those children's mother: but what else can happen, our eyes said, once we have all dispersed to various parts of the world? "What can we do, what can we do," the rhythm of my day breathed. So on the morning when they left Lahore, for the pink house on the hill, there was terror in my hands as I held them one by one: "Child's mind, do not forget, I am your mother's sister," my fingers begged. But as they drove away, I turned to see Tillat raise her head in the anguish of such despairing tears that I knew it, then, that they were lost.

Javed has remarried now, and when I visit Pakistan, Ifat's

children look at me shyly, at this strange aunt belonging to an era before their lives capsized: their mother's younger sister, older now than their mother was when she was taken from them. In some police station in Lahore a file of an unsolved murder from 1980 lies forgotten, or perhaps completely lost. But we have managed to live with ourselves, it seems, making a habit of loss. "The thought most killing to me," I told Tillat, "is—if Ifat could be asked—how firmly she would swear that we would never let the children go." Tillat winced. "We did not have a choice, Sara. What could we do—live with them in Javed's house after what had been said?" We shivered at the contemplation of that old terrain. "I think Ifat would feel most compassionate for us," Tillat murmured, "you know what she was like . . . compassionate . . . " I shook my head. "But to such an extreme that she would probably have imagined that we would be capable of a most radically compassionate act." "Yes, she was extreme," she said. And, suddenly, we smiled at some moment of Ifat's extremity: we did not need to tell them to each other but let those two moments rise between us like a tiny replication of her aura. It was nearly with us, that astonishing radiance, in the way that something you have dreamed the night before can come flashing in and out of your morning, leaving you astonishing, "What was it that I dreamed?"

I like to imagine that there is a space for improvident angels, the ones who wish to get away from too much light. There, a company of Ifat lie, arms across their foreheads, such an intensely familiar thought that it brings tears of delight to the grave eyes of god.

# WHAT MAMMA KNEW

My mother could not do without Jane Austen. This I had always known, long before I watched her face wear like the binding of a book, that creases its leather into some soft texture and acquires a subtle spine free of gilt, knowing better than openly to announce its title. For her preferences were there in every room, putting words into my mouth before my taste buds had acquired a means to cope with their suggestion: I had conducted a steady parlance with the names of books years prior to my reading of what those names embraced and held as secrets from me. Titles with a proper name in them were easiest, so I never had much difficulty with respecting the privacy of *Tom Jones, Madame Bovary.* I next felt reassured by every definite article that came my way, because even my own books—storybooks—knew how to tell me in an uncomplicated fashion what it meant to read upon a printed page "The End." So I did not mind when I spelled out to myself *The Mystery*—even when it then became the possession of such a haunting name as Edwin Drood—as long as mystery was contained by a *The* that declared some mastery of narrative. The titles that eluded context were the ones that troubled me: *Persuasion*, I would read—a whole book about a single word!—or *Beyond the Pleasure Principle*—what did it mean, to write a book beyond what it was about? Troubled and entranced, I was pleased to have my mother lead me through those shelves and see the pleasure it conferred on her when she told me, contemplatively, "Yes, now you're old enough to read Jane Austen."

Afternoons were reading time, since the obligatory siesta of the East, constructed to appease a summer sun, barely changes character during those brief winter months when the brilliance of the sky brings cool pleasure. In every season each day was built around the expectation of a secluded afternoon, it being useful for a day to know that a space of time will arrive when the hours need not behave as day but can lie down, abstracted. My mother's children would retire to their various beds with books: each afternoon the house was quiet with reading. Then the day could rise again, inspired by the prospect of the night and ready to resume the task of company. I liked this segmented quality to time, this pause—surely something in each day should give it pause—the reintroduction through which day gave way to evening and then to the workings of the night. But we had to rise early, start thinking early, in order to enjoy those afternoons: I begged to be allowed to sleep as long as possible, savoring each minute of my sleep. Finally my mother would go out into the courtyard and call up my name, which would reach me reluctantly, breaking through rest's liquidity to say, "Mair Jones, your mother, is standing outside and calling up to you, asking you to wake and become this thing, your name." An overalliterated name, I thought as I got up, this thing that I have to be.

I liked the old campus of the university where my mother taught. Its crazy commingling of Victoriana with the kind of architecture the Victorians thought we Indians liked was pleasing to me, with its curious lion-colored stone and vast, aging interiors. Those massive domes and courtyards sit opposite the red museum and the court, just at the point where the Mall is about to trail off toward the Ravi River, making the transition from British Lahore to Mughal Lahore. The university intersects the two, looking out at Kim's Gun and the museum where Kipling's father worked, turning its back on the intricacies of the Anarkali bazaar, named after the dancing girl that Jāhangīr is fabled to have loved. She was bricked alive into her grave as punishment for having solicited a prince's love, but at least it was not a lonely grave, lying at the heart of the getting and spending of Lahore's busiest bazaar. When I first entered the university, the thought of being—in such a literal way—my mother's student was strange to me, putting us both in a novel setting, over books. She seemed subdued to see me sitting in her public world, as though one had leaked into the other in some dreamwork, and, to the voice that had roused me an hour earlier, my name became an intensely private thing: "Yes, Fawzia?" "Yes, Huma?" she would say, and then, looking at me, "Yes?" But she forgot my presence once, thus teaching me the rare pleasure that can attend a mother's forgetfulness. For she was teaching Jane Austen. Whenever was there such a perfect match, I thought entranced, between teacher and the task? Task and teacher seemed wedded as a voice marries thought, making it impossible to discern at which point one revealed the other's reticence. I was working at the theater in those days, dropping in at the univeristy only when I had a chance, but now had quickly to reschedule all my rehearsal hours to accommodate Jane Austen. "What," I exclaimed, "rehearse right now, and miss my mother teaching *Emma?*" Then, as I watched that face light up, a smile quickening its voice even when she was not smiling, there was curious recognition in her familiarity of face. "Oh," I realized, "so it's not just Emma. Mamma's daughters also bring her joy."

I recalled the posture of that discourse, its reserve, when last summer my sister Nuz turned to me and said, "Mair was *To the Lighthouse* for me—she was Mrs. Ramsay." Nuz loves to pay a compliment, although it is a love fraught with risk to her: her eyes watch anxiously the unfolding of her praise, saying—even before it's done— "No, I have not said it: this is not enough." I smiled at her analogy, which pleased me, but told her that somehow I would say my mother was more invisible, more difficult to discern. "Mair was beautiful!" Nuz answered, bridling. I laughed. "So much so that she never wore it or anything upon her sleeve—did you notice that?—her sleeves were always empty." This was true, there always being around my mother hints of the capacity of space, as though each time she moved, she made interstices, neutral regions of low color quite ravishing to anyone who, as daughter, was observer. For she moved in observation to a degree that caught my breath, made it draw back to create more space and murmur, "I am observing what it means to be in observation." During the years of her existence, I did not altogether understand this gravity, this weightlessness, she carried with her. But then, I did not teach. Now that I do, I know that great sobriety of tone betokens the bearing of a stately teacher whose step is always measuring out what she sees as the edges of this great impossibility, of what it means to teach.

Sometimes, when I feel burdened by this baldest prose—I lived too long with the man of the hairless head—and tyrannized by the structure of a simple sentence, it does me good to recollect how quietly my mother measured out her dealings with impossible edges. What can I do but tell the same story again and yet again, as my acknowledgment of how dangerous it is to live in plot? What else was Mamma teaching when she passed me with a story that was always falling short? For something has to fall, as a day writes itself out into the more hectic writing of the night, and I am glad to be imbecile enough to wish it had been mine and not my mother's head. "You can't change people, Sara," she once told me, watching with compassion my crazy efforts on that behalf. How she would smile and shake her head, to see my complete regression into a woman who does not care for character at all and wants to change only the plot. Was it because she had so many children that she exempted herself from similar pedantic tricks, preferring, of necessity, to configurate her mind around what need not be said, much as she congregated all our fussy eating habits around a meal? I would not like to be responsible for the way so many people choose to eat and not to eat, for even when I teach I sometimes think I fall into a lazy way of talking as though there were simply a bunch of equally fed bodies in front of me, not stopping in my haste to listen and to differentiate. It makes me realize something of my mother's concentration in her home, of her perpetual attention to the assembly of our stories, which let her learn the limits of our private tastes, what each of us could and could not eat. She was too courteous to write as I am writing now, thrusting down the gullets of my intimates each day the selfsame meal!

"You learned to talk very early, Sara," Mamma told me of my forgotten past. "You were so interested in sentences." It made me the quaintest baby that she had—as an infant I was absorbed with grammar before I had fully learned the names of things, which caused a single slippage in my nouns: I would call a marmalade a squirrel, and I'd call a squirrel a marmalade. Today I can understand the impulse and would very much like to call sugar an opossum; an antelope, tea. To be engulfed by grammar after all is a tricky prospect, and a voice deserves to declare its own control in any way it can, asserting that in the end it is an inventive thing. Think how much a voice gives way to plot when it learns to utter the names of the people that it loves: picture looking at Peter and saying, "Peter"; picture picking up the telephone to Anita's voice and crying out, "Nina!" How can syntax hold around a name? Picture my mother on the beautiful old campus of the Punjab University looking straight at her daughter and saying, "Yes?"

During my years at the university, I became quite accustomed to the way people would walk up to me and say, "I love Mrs. Suleri!" "I understand the sensation," I'd smile in reply. And the reason that they loved her made me smile further, for Mrs. Suleri's demeanor was most enchanting to the world at precisely the moment when it announced, "It is not necessary to be liked." Her composure held this compelling thought at bay, as though the greatest lucidity she could conduct was to say silently, "Leave it, let it go away, the grammatical construction of what it is to like and be liked!" She looked lovely with announcement: "Think what you will liberate—your days to extraordinary ideas—if you could cut away the sentence with which you wish to be liked!" Without even knowing what they had heard, her students' faces would suffuse with gratitude, conscious that some kindness had occurred while their understanding was elsewhere. And so with devotion they would leave her presence; with devotion they'd return. Mamma, who was always irritated by the unthinking structure of adulation, would smile a little absently at them, concealing her annoyance in something else, some slight gesture of vagueness or distraction. For trying to make people think beyond devotion made of her a particularly absentminded woman, one who hid the precision of her judgment in a dispersed aura that spread throughout each room she inhabited, so that finally her students were not to blame for breathing happily in such lucid air. What lesson could she hope to teach, when she was sitting there before them, her face ravishing with some forgotten thought?

It was always hard to keep her in one place, make her stay with you in a way that let you breathe, "Now she has no secrets." She seemed to live increasingly outside the limits of her body, until I felt I had no means of holding her, lost instead in the reticence of touch. I could tell that she was still teaching me, I sensed throughout a day the perpetual gravity with which my mother taught, but I was baffled by her lesson: if I am to break out of the structure of affection, I asked her silently, then what is the idiom in which I should live? She would not tell me, but even today—as I struggle with the quaintness of the task I've set myself, the obsolescence of these quirky little tales—I can feel her spirit shake its head to tell me, "Daughter, unplot yourself; let be." But I could not help the manner in which my day was narrative, quite happy to let Mamma be that haunting word at which narrative falls apart. Like the secluded hours of afternoon, my mother would retract and disappear, leaving my story suspended until she reemerged. I think it was a burden to her to be so central to that tale: she certainly seemed most full of her own quietude when we let her wander by herself up and down the garden, picking up a pebble or a twig to murmur, "Look . . ." I so loved to watch her when she was alone and also so much liked to be her companion on those strolls that it always wrenched me, as though some great pleasure had to be renounced whether I watched or walked. "Mamma," I once asked her tentatively as we walked up and down an evening garden, "Do you need to spend more time away from us, from this?" gesturing at the house and all the duties it implied. "No," she said judiciously, "all of you are quite sufficient to me," adding with a slightly rueful smile, "You keep me entertained." It brought quick guilt to me, when I could suddenly sense how many stories sat around her secrets, clamoring for the attention of her face. There were the five of us, and Dadi, and students, and the cook, and Halima the cleaning woman with her sick son. And then there was also my father.

How can I bring them together in a room? My plot feels most dangerous to me when I think of bringing them together. Can I even recollect how they sat together in a room, that most reticent woman and that most demanding man? Something in me wishes to recoil, to say let it be hid, the great exhaustion of that image. Papa's powerful discourse would surround her night and day—when I see her in his room, she is always looking down, gravely listening! They were rhetorically so different, the two of them, always startling each other with the difference of their speech: no wonder their children grew up with such a crazy language; words that blustered out their understatement, phrases ironic of their scorn. To Papa's mode of fearsome inquiry we married Mamma's expression of secret thought, making us—if nothing else—faithful in physiognomy. For we were glad enough to sing epithalamiums for the way that history wed silence, almost freshly, every day. Oh, of course there was dignity in that incongruous union, in the lengthy habit of that unlikely pair, reminding me of how much they must have lost and suffered in order to become habitual. I could sometimes see it on my mother's face: not judgment but a slightly sorrowful acknowledgment that said, "It was for this," as she watched my father talking; "For this," as we came bantering into the room. She found him moving—his very doggedness, committedness, a moving thing—long after she had glided off into a realm beyond the noncomittal, a creature of such translucent thought that my father could not follow, could not see. But he respected her almightily, fearing the ill-judgment she was far too courteous to give, so that daily he would watch her finish his latest article to ask her anxiously, "How does it read?" "It reads well, Zia," she'd say, which—once one had pushed through his baffling single-mindedness—it very often did. I was bone-tired after ten years of reading articles in galley proofs and needed to put continents between newsprint and my mind: my mother lived through thirty years of the daily production of that print, the daily necessity of sympathy.

"Mairi," said my father to my mother, "what is the greatest thing you've done in your life?"—hardly my mother's favorite lingo, but Pip was in a chatty mood and liked to talk of greatness. She looked at him, restrained. Her restraint said clearly: "Why, enduring you, you impossible, you moving man!" But to protect him, she added, "Oh, my children, I would say." "And I—I have not done one great thing, but I saw greatness, during the struggle for Pakistan." And then he launched off into one of his familiar rhapsodies—not too different in tone, I'd hazard, from the ones that felt so strange and moving to her in postwar London, when she was a girl. I saw the crossing of patience on her face, making her at once abstracted, faraway. To mock him would be too simple: he demanded to be mocked, and had enough detractors as it was, proliferating through his day. So my mother gave him the seriousness of her concern, following the self-interruptions of his talk to say, "I see, I see." I think she had expected him to age out of defiance, as had she, for in her defiance dropped away to leave her in some new simplicity: when it did not in her husband, she took note, and said: "I see." As I watched their conversation, I was struck. No wonder my mother sought to teach me, with oblique urgency, the necessity of what it means to live beyond affection. No wonder she said to me—startlingly, incongruously—"You can't change people, Sara." For when her sympathy was in its bloom, I saw, how hard its fresh-faced patience must have worked to compensate for each bad dream! Why, she had tried to change my father, I realized; she tried, until she could not try.

But now I am dejected, as though I had been commissioned to write a piece of melancholy music for which the only payment was my own melancholic chords. Somehow it will not grip me, the telling of this tale, not with my mother's aura hovering nearby to remind me of one of her most clear announcements: "Child, I will not grip." Intensity of any kind made her increasingly uneasy, and as a consequence she worked at all hours to keep her connection with her children at low tide—still a powerfully magnetic thing, but at an ebbing tide, so that there was always a ghostly stretch of neither here nor there between her sea and our shore. "Mother," I would sometimes exclaim in raw exasperation, "You are too retrograde, you have no right to recede so far!" "Would you have me possess you, then?" her manner quietly replied. "Shall I stay close till you are marshland, admiring the bulrushes sprouting from your brains? Must I search among those bulrushes for some baby Moses of my children's minds, when surely I by now have seen all that I should of similar labor?—No, child, I will not grip." And so today it saddens me to think I could be laying hands upon the body of her water as though it were reducible to fragrance, as though

I intensified her vanished ways into some expensive salt. Flavor of my infancy, my mother, still be food: I want my hunger as it always was, neither flesh nor fowl!

So let me tell us all some happy story. "But does she spend too much time alone?" I heard my mother wonder to my father as I walked unexpectedly into their London bedroom. My father was in bed, at bliss, lying in bed surrounded by newspapers. He turned to me with huge concern, holding my seven-year-old shoulders to exclaim aghast, "Sara, Mamma tells me that you have no friends!" My mother looked pained in her tact. She shook her head and sighed; then she looked down. "Ifat has so many friends!" he added. It was true that my sister was radiant with company, and so I thought about his analogy, until a happy formulation crossed my mind: "It's because Ifat's white, and I am brown," I suggested brightly. I knew that I had given him, essentialized, a scrupulous rendition of school-ground politics, but Papa the politician was outraged. Ifat, who could pass as English, had one hurdle less to cross than I did in our Chiswick school—she and I had talked about it many times. But Papa could not stomach such bald fact, launching instead into a long and passionate speech about the ancient civilization that inhered in my genes, about how steadily I should walk in such proud pigmentation. "You are my wheaten daughter," he declared, "wheaten, and most beautiful!" Oh dear, I thought, looking down. How could I tell him that I was only trying to locate a difference, a fact that shaped my day much as weather did, the wet chill of an English spring? I had not the language to face up to his strong talk, and so looked down instead, almost as though he were right to assume that I had felt ashamed, inferior. "Never call color by its proper name," I told myself, at seven. My mother did not say a word, but later that evening when I told her it was quite cold in the garden, "How truthful you are, Sara," she said with bright approval, "What a truthful girl you are!"

For my mother loved to look at us in race. I have watched her pick up an infant's foot—Irfan's, perhaps, or Tillat's—

with an expression of curiously sealed wonder, as though her hand had never felt so full as when she held her infants' feet. They were Asiatic, happiest when allowed to be barefoot or to walk throughout the world with a leather thong between their toes—a moving thought, to Mamma. Sometimes when we ran into a room she would look at the fascination of race in each of us, darting like red foxes round her room. "And to this," her wonder said, "to these, I am the vixen?" When we made something, drew a picture that she liked, there was again a moment of glad surprise upon her face at the tangibility of what lay before her. I assume her mind was so preoccupied with all our tales, so abstracted with them, that the times when we became suddenly tangible were a form of recompense to her. Then she loved the way what her mother called our "heathen names" became bodily events, calling attention to the accessibility of our difference. My father would look at his children with an equal delight, but somehow he seemed to notice only beauty, whereas my mother seemed subdued with awe at the commingling of color that with our bodies we flung onto her, comminglings in which she had colluded to produce. And so there was a trace of sadness in her welcome, as though the aftermath of joy suggested fears that asked her, "What will happen to these pieces of yourself—you, and yet not you—when you dispatch them into the world? Have you made sufficient provision for their extraordinary shadows?" The question made her retreat.

Where did she go when she retreated? Often away from us and into her own childhood, back to some Welsh moment that served to succor her when duty felt too great. She much admired her father, who used to sing: on some holiday mornings I would not wake to the sound of my mother calling up my name but instead to the sound of her privacy with some piece of music, her singing to it rather than to me. There was always some filial obligation that she paid in the pleasure she took to sit down at his piano, so when I stood at the top of the stairs and watched her play, I could see her spine swaying with loyalty. She was paying a compliment to some lost moment of her life, and I felt startled to observe such privacy. What great good fortune has flooded through this day, I would think, and then go slowly down the stairs, measuring my steps to the weaving movement of her body. When Tillat awoke I could see on her face too a sleepy gratitude, savoring the luxury of such a waking. For that span of time she was not my mother to me but a creature that had left itself and caught up with its voice, in voice's way of exceeding the limits of its body, so that the air we breathed was strung with secrets, luminous and sheathed.

Today, when I listen to that haunting Punjabi poet Baba Bulhe Shah being sung, he transports me to the days when I would wake to hear my mother sing. There could hardly be more different music, hers and his, but something in his cadence has to do with her: I feel perplexed at the incongruity of this connection, but when I listen to the old Punjabi poem *Hir Ranjha* being sung, I curiously enough think of my mother. The story is simple: Hir loves Ranjha and is separated from him, sent off to live in a strange tribe where, after much to-do, she dies, thus also killing Ranjha. At one point in the tale, however, Hir looks at the strangers that surround her and sings out: "No one can call me Hir; I have named Ranjha so many times that I have become his name; I have become him by myself; you cannot call me Hir." Now the passion in that voice is not my mother's—she was always wary of overpassionate tones—but in my mind she is linked to the gravity of Hir's posture: surely she would be familiar with that trick of mind with which Hir told the world that she had become someone else's name and now was Hir no longer? The romance of it has little to do with Mamma—where she rises gravely before my eyes is when Hir is living in a stranger's village, moving in the decorum of a repudiated name.

What an act of concentration it must have required, after all, the quick conversion through which Mair Jones became Surraya Suleri! She had to redistribute herself through several new syllables, realigning her sense of locality until—within the span of a year—she was ready to leave London and become a citizen of Pakistan. How literal-minded of her. Did she really think that she could assume the burden of empire, that if she let my father colonize her body and her name she would perform some slight reparation for the race from which she came? Could she not see that his desire for her was quickened with empire's ghosts, that his need to possess was a clear index of how he was still possessed? The globe was a bigger place in 1947, so her journey must have been arduous when she rose to put behind her every circuit of familiarity she had ever known. She left for what she imagined was a brand-new nation, a populace filled with the energy of independence, and arrived to discover an ancient landscape, feudal in its differentiation of tribes, and races, and tongues. For a woman who liked to speak precisely, she must have hated her sudden linguistic incompetence: languages surrounded her like a living space, insisting that she live in other people's homes. My mother was a guest, then, a guest in her own name, living in a resistant culture that would not tell her its rules: she knew there must be many rules and, in compensation, developed the slightly distracted manner of someone who did not wish to be breaking rules of which she was ignorant. For what choice had that world but to be resistant? The touching good faith of her Pakistani passport could hardly change the fact that even as my mother thought she was arriving, she actually had returned. There were centuries' worth of mistrust of Englishwomen in their eyes when they looked at her who chose to come after the English should have been gone: what did she mean by saying, "I wish to be part of you"? Perhaps, they feared, she mocked.

Abnegating power is a powerful thing to do, as my mother must have learned to admit: in the eyes of Pakistan, her repudiation of race gave her a disembodied Englishness that was perhaps more threatening than if she had come with a desire to possess. In the necessary amnesia of that era, colonial history had to be immediately annulled, put firmly in the past; remembrance was now contraband in a world still learning to feel unenslaved. What could that world do with a woman who called herself a Pakistani but who looked suspiciously like the past it sought to forget? Then my mother learned the ironies of nationhood—of what can and cannot be willed—when she had to walk through her new context in the shape of a memory erased. Involved with his impetuous politics, my father probably did not notice the aura that now surrounded his wife, or perhaps he thought it was his need of her that gave Mair her new tread. She learned to live apart, then—apart even from herself—growing into that curiously powerful disinterest in owning, in belonging, which years later would make her so clearly tell her children, "Child, I will not grip." She let commitment and belonging become my father's domain, learning instead the way of walking with tact on other people's land.

No, it is not merely devotion that makes my mother into the land on which this tale must tread. I am curious to locate what she knew of the niceties that living in someone else's history must entail, of how she managed to dismantle that other history she was supposed to represent. Furthermore, I am interested to see how far any tale can sustain the name of "mother," or whether such a name will have to signify the severance of story. Her plot therefore must waver: it must weave in her own manner of sudden retreating, as though I could almost see her early surprise when she found herself in Pakistan, on someone else's land. I, who have watched her read a book, and teach it, should be able to envisage the surrendering of black and white behind her reading of the land. No wonder she felt nuanced, when her progeny was brown.

For Mamma, in whom affection became so soon a figure for obsolescence, must have learned years before I was conceivable in thought what I have discovered only recently, that love renders a body into history. Like litmus, apprehended love can only turn historical, making of desire a social nicety, companionable. "I must say, Mamma," I said to her as we went walking in companionable conversation, "It was most incongruous, most perverse of you to take to Pip." She looked amused. "You must not minimize my affection for him," she replied with slight reproof. "But you're the one who says it doesn't count!" "Oh," said Mamma vaguely, "as conduct I suppose it counts," and then turned toward some nearby shrub, but I pulled her back into our talk. "If affection's conduct, then what's history?" I asked her, curious. ". . . Bearing . . . " she answered, vaguer than ever, ". . . even posture, perhaps . . . " "But that's just like squirrel and marmalade!" "Indeed it is," she laughed. And so I let her trail off away from conversation, unable still to grasp why—despite her vaguenesses, retreats—her finesse would always feel so sound.

How would I define her soundness? By the time I came to consciousness, she had long since intuited the rules of Pakistan—those hidden laws that people would not tell her—and had come to terms with the ones she could and could not keep. If she was attentive to my father, courteous with his intensities, his ragings, then her attentiveness to Pakistan was an even greater strain: her intimacy with place and way grew habitual with the years but never changed her habit of seeming to announce, "It is good of you to let me live—in my own way—among you." She even had that habit with her children! Why would not her manner of announcement register as propitiatory, defensive? Because it was not acquisitive, perhaps? I cannot say, but Mamma moved through Pakistan with a curious relaxation that seemed unencumbered by any judgment—an odd claim to make about such a judicious woman, but she certainly appeared to suggest that the possibility of adding herself to anything was irrelevant to her. By the same token, she did not fear subtraction; her method of exchange functioned at the greatest possible remove from the structure of a bargain. Since the world she inhabited was so committedly fond of the language of bargaining, she became to that community a creature of unique and unclassifiable discourse. Her students, for instance, told their families, "I think she is a saint." But when such tales reached us, they caused my mother some annoyance and her children considerable glee. I immediately suggested that we set up some small trade, a stall in the Anarkali bazaar, specializing in saintly portraits and other sundry charms: we could call the shop The Effects of Mrs. Suleri (Personal and Otherwise). "You can't treat people's feelings as though they were items on a marketplace," she chided me, adding, in her habit of secret logic, "I know how the human body is made."

Her logic was indeed a secret. "The only trouble with being female in Pakistan," Ifat complained, years later, "is that it allows for two possible modes of behavior—either you can be sweet and simple, or you can be cold and proud." "No wonder they found Mamma difficult to decipher, then," I agreed, "whose coldness was so sweet . . . " "As tactful as ice in water," Ifat added passionately, "and as sweet!" Tact, we knew, was far more difficult to define than a simple moral structure such as sanctity, and for us to place her meant we had to come to terms with what tact had to do with the idea of distraction. It was her element: sometimes when I watched her face, I would realize that she was not distracted from any one thing or in the direction of another—in her, distraction unalloyed was simply her habit of possible serenity. Out of that vagueness floated the precision of her judgment, and we were never able to determine which came first. Was precision the fodder for her vacant peace, or was it vacancy that allowed her to be lucid? She felt apologetic that she could not explain her manner more exactly to her children, who on occasion were exasperated with their need to understand. I think she was too unconvinced by the stability of logic to help us on this score, though she was sorry, she regretted to me, to give us such denial. "You don't deny us, Mamma," I told her—it was important that she know we did not feel denied. "You must be just as you are, and we must discover why." "Why?" she asked me, gently, in the poignant structure of a question that is really saying, "Let things be." "Oh, you must have had a child for each of your lost obsessions," I muttered, "so now it's just our business to work out which one we are." "Which one?" "Which obsession." When she looked at me, her eyes were kind: I had to stop talking, then, uncertain whether we were close to some forbidden boundary or had crossed it long ago. For, with the years, our conversations would become more dangerous, ready to say so much that they leapt back in fear of distressing the illusion of lucidity.

Oddly, in her aftermath that single conversation haunts me. Could we, I sometimes wonder just before I sleep—in the vagrant clarity of thoughts that fight not to be dreams—work out which one of us was which? Could it be an indelicacy in me, to so catalog what she kept quietly hidden? But still, the making of such patterns has a magic to it, a pull I won't resist: Ifat was my mother's lost obsession with being as passionate as my father; Shahid, her hunger after gentleness; I could be her need to think in sentences; and Tillat, an obsession with strange patience; Irfan, her urge to be ignorant and pure. And Nuz would then become—since Nuz was always in the room with us—her hankering for the child she never had. For in the curious waiting of every pregnancy I've witnessed crouches doubt: what child am I relinquishing, maternity must ask, to give this growing thing my full attention? What missing child will be the summation of my children? The notion that she could have lacked a child is entrancing to me, and so I must reconfigure my thoughts and then begin again. Ifat was her lost obsession with beauty; Shahid, her nostalgia for the good; Tillat . . . but now I am asleep . . . and then, Irfan.

Have I mentioned that I loved her face? I liked its posture of disinterest, the way she did not really fret over the wearing and tearing of her lovely things as they were shipped from town to town, getting lost and broken on the way. In a similar fashion, she took no notice of the beautiful wearing of her face, around which fatigue would register only as the burden of intelligence. "One's aesthetic changes," Mamma murmured to me, "once one has a child." I smiled at that: one, maybe, but two? three? four? I wondered, and did not even need the rhetorical thrust of the fifth. But it made me reconsider the possible location of her inattention, of her lucidity: we were accustomed to assuming that my father's historical posture prevailed heavily on our home, but this could be our slight error. What if we questioned their joint apportioning of duty, looked again at what was literature, what history? I recall my father waking my mother up to say expressly, "Mairi, look at the beauty—the balance—of this front page!" He made each front page fit into his control of the aesthetic of his history. My mother, however, let history seep, so that, miraculously, she had no language in which to locate its functioning but held it rather as a distracted manner sheathed about her face, a scarf. "Mamma was more political . . . " I essayed the idea to Tillat. "She did not have to put it into print—it was the sheet in which she slept . . . " So of course she never noticed the imprint on her face as it wore, for she was that imprint: she was her own dust before her bones had dreamed that they could crumble.

We, her children, somehow must have sensed that she intended to become herself in every available manner, be one with her own history, her dust, in a way that made us just a moment in her successive transformation. And so we made ourselves complicit in her habit of hidden variety, glad to be brash foils to her neutrality of color. "I will be blistering daylight," I decided, "an exhausting thing to be, as long as such a posture gives to her the region of the afternoon." "I will be the flamboyance of the night," declared Ifat, "if only she would show me just one sentence of what her afternoon sleep must read!" And then we traded all the time, I taking from Tillat for a day her dogged quietude, she from me the publicity of a protection that knew it must fail, all of us never sure that what we needed to buy today is what yesterday we sold. "Well, she makes her living by being a teacher," our eyes said to each other, and then smiled. We were the classroom in which she had to walk and say with some reluctance,

"Take disappointment, child, eat disappointment from me."
I saw us shift, uneasy to be furniture to such a discourse.
"Since I must make you taste, let me put gravel on your
tongues, those rasping surfaces that years ago I watered! If
you cannot, will not, live—as I insist—outside historical
affection, then I must be for you the living lesson of the costs
of history." She hated such a statement, which was hard,
quite hard on all of us, collaborating in the parameters of
where the giving of learning began, against the taking of
teaching.

Where are the lines that must be drawn between the
teacher and what can be taught? In my mother, distracted-
ness erased those lines, allowing instead for lucidity to take
control of context. And so we could not help but ask silently:
Is it fair, Mamma, is it fair that you have reached a point
where you no longer bother to differentiate between what the
world imagines you must be and what you are? Is that it, what
you are saying? For she would not discriminate, other than to
enact for us her vital promise that we would know disappointment. As students it was hard for us to know so much about a
teacher, about her responsibility. Will she ever draw a line, I
wondered, between lesson and herself? Were we the ones to
state the boundaries, to make the limit, which is what her
lesson said? I hated drawing a limit. I hated my own youth,
when I watched the ways my mother sought to teach us of
disappointment, and could not help but grieve, "Oh, look,
she disappoints."

Now fabrication fails me, and such fatigue signifies a
possible alternative to accomplishment. Against the quality
of her instruction, I must insist that I have said it all, said
everything that I must say. She smiles slightly at my pugilistic
manner and trails off before I have courage enough to ask her
leave—Mamma, marmalade, squirrel—to apprehend her
name.

# SAVING DAYLIGHT

Each year, an hour gained. Because I never tampered with the clocks in Pakistan, these last ten years feel bold to me, for they have put me in the realm of daylight saving and made me mistress of my time. That evening in October still remains an oddity to me, suggesting a moment of keen transaction, until I am not sure that I can grasp what I keep repeating, "You must put back the clock an hour tonight." The sudden twilights of the East denied such duty from our day—never said to us, "Put back the clock"—and thus did not unleash into our time the strangeness of an hour that seems uncertain of its own numerical arrangement: is it something wastrel, gay, or does it assert peculiarly sad thrift? For the expectancy of winter aches, makes cavity, and yet is still expectant. I recall the triumph that the monsoons bring, those rains that come to kill the summer sun, in the annual peace that falls on me in New Haven each time I notice it is no longer dark at five and the air sighs out, "another winter done." Soon, I think, we will put the clock forward, obliterate one April hour, and the day will make a startling leap into expansive evenings, creating ample setting for lucid conversation. What times of old luxury I have known in something like the miraculous length of evening in an English summer, a lag of time so much in tune with the spacious speech of Shahid! Or perhaps his voice is elsewhere, in another arena of possible accustom, sitting in a garden with my father talking through night's stillness, the total stillness of a summer in Lahore. The garden is still full with people and voices, bodies waiting for the rain and its sharp release of fragrance when it puts water on their dust, in order that they may sigh aloud, "another summer done." I, in some other era of negotiation with my clock, own now a different idiom in which to mention respite: "anther summer," sighs my father; "another winter," echo I.

The world, it seems, is fraught with bitter seasons. Either beckoning or leaving some intensity, the month that we call March has totally changed character for me, from the time when a day, two days, would replicate in abbreviated form the smell, the feel of summer. You must not feel elated, I would warn myself—but still, I was elated—at the idea of the single-mindedness of summer: something is coming to strip us to the bone, I thought, something to make our thoughts live in interior spaces. Odd, that the prospect of intensity can be exhilarating, but it was with a shiver of exhilaration that I would make March my time of preparation for a span of months designed to make me work quite hard if I planned to match my spirit with its own. But now the time is one of curious relaxation, a month when spirit can sit down abstracted, saying "Never mind, never mind—this is not snow but merely snow's remembrance, a reassurance that precipitation ends." Summer turns its tables on me now, and March arrives to tell me things are inside out, that I no longer need a moment to prepare. And though the month brought twice to me days of wicked occasion, some simple principle of understanding makes me recognize that I have not mourned in March.

Memory is not the work of mourning. I used to think it was a matter of a catalog, some list that I could draw with loving neatness, since neatness is the attribute of tenderness. And so, each year when Dale and Fawzi flood my home with flowers to commemorate my sister or my mother, I know at last that what those flowers represent is not an attitude available for my adoption: instead, with curiosity, I watch the tulips curl, stiffen, and collapse, performing on their own behalf the sufficiency of mourning. Ifat was probably more compassionate to herself than I could ever be, in the quick second when she said yes, now surely she would die. It makes me smile. To mourn, perhaps, is simply to prolong a posture of astonishment, like the astonishing posture in which my grandmother found herself shortly before she died. Apparently when in her nineties she was dying, frail, my brother Irfan was deputed to transport her from Lahore to Islamabad: he chose to take a train, since Pakistan is still a country that takes railways seriously. Such commitment makes of stations, however, a seething mass of life: once they had reached Rawalpindi and Irfani had looked first at my grandmother and then at the density of bodies all around him, he decided that he had no choice but to pick my Dadi up and, holding her above his head, go running through those bodies like a coolie, crying, *"Jan dus!*—Give way! Give way!" Light and tiny Dadi, the luggage on that coolie's head, sent wraiths of wails toward the ceiling: "Irfan, Irfan, Irfan."

I wrote about my grandmother once and, having written such a tale, thought to use it as a surrogate for the letters that I owed to intimates, those who—in the manner of old friends—had fallen by the wayside into mere remembrance. Such people are a danger to your life, becoming as they do indistinguishable from invention, friends that you idly muse you wished to have—until your brain gets up and chides, "This one, you had." One such a friend was David L., intimate and succor of my youth, with whom a habit of exchange was in arrest: I wished somehow to rejuvenate our old sense of it, the barter of significance. I remembered the commerce of watching David in conversation with an artisan at work at restoring the surfaces of the Wazir Khan Mosque in old Lahore. David spoke in Urdu; the artisan replied in English. "It is fresco," the old man kept saying, "I am doing fresco." "I am doing fresco, David," I wrote, unmindful of whether he recollected the occasion. "But who are you writing for?" he wrote back, "What are you still protecting?" I thought a while . . . oh yes, I understood, I know what David tries to teach: the proper names of pain.

A David pain looks at what you are and seems to say, "Is that it? Is that all?" A Dale pain invokes the proximity of sympathy, which must veer back from consolation, since your woe is her own. A Tillat pain folds back into illusions of serenity, putting that bonny girl into silences of what cannot be said. Shahid's pain insists his sensibility is done; an Anita pain suggests that you have reneged on the duty of sensibility. And in his day, Tom would bring a pain that said, "What can love do to stave it off, my notion of the brutality of what it means to be civilized? Must I, for you, interrupt the burden of my effort?" A Fawzi pain insists she must be a child, so that as she engenders children's love, she watches horrified and whispers: "I am one of you—do not give me love so soon, not yet!" A Papa pain glances as a stranger would upon the thing it loved; Mamma pain suggests the immorality of absence. Nuzzi's pain draws on her bravery: something must be suffering, each time that she laughs. And an Ifat pain inhered in the hilarity of her brooding manner, the one that darkly looked up through her brightness, saying, "Love me, while you can." Idiotic girl, to have needed apocalypse to allow her being: look at the price that we are paying now!

For whom are you writing, David asked me. For the jewels and tiny serpents hidden in such names as yours, I thought. And so he set me pondering about the notion of nomenclature inside these quirky little tales, brittle homes to put upon the mollusk of a name. But surely it was preferable to pick up an empty shell, a structure bleached with the promise that it once was home? I cannot help it, David, if my names sound hollow to you, residences that you must condemn: to me, they are the words most shaped like beds, and I am glad to find them empty, attendant on my rest. I have

173

always liked to see a vacant space intact—a room disinterested in seeming furnished—which surely shows the influence of growing up in houses built around courtyards, designed in a world where people pray in mosques. I still miss it, the necessity of openness that puts a courtyard in the middle of a house and makes rooms curl around it, so that each bedroom is but a door away from the seclusion of the sky. In summers, too, we slept beneath the stars: curious sensation, to lie on a rope-bed and watch the sky, until sleep comes as confirmation of the magnificent irrelevance of beauty.

After Ifat had been emptied, the world made my father pay a gratuitous price. It taught us that the language of investigation is a very literal thing, insisting that there is an inside after all to each exterior. Why, they asked him, had he so adamantly refused to let them perform an autopsy on her, why had he insisted that she be buried intact instead, in the grave-space that he'd thought would be his own? "Because," he answered, sullen pain upon his face, "I could not let them violate the dignity of her body." He behaved, of course, with rectitude, as he always did in moments of extremity, and we were the first to tell him, "You did right." What secrets could they hope to find at such an opening? If there were secrets, they would sheen in peace, until they melted into tenderness at being made part, again, of my mother's dust. "Haven't they read," I grumbled, "Aesop on the goose that laid the golden eggs?" For Ifat's gold was in her speech, in language that reflected like a radiance from her: they would find nothing at her interior. My father did not deserve to be so questioned, making him look up with anger, when he had to spell out such obviousness—"*I* India, *F* Frank, *A* Apple, *T* Thomas"—in a sullen pain. Today, the angle of his face returns to me as I wonder at the configuration I discern: David, asking what do you still need to protect, to hide; Papa, his lion's head looking up like a beast in pain; Ifat, being put away intact at last; and I, combing through a day for some injunction of what is possible, impossible, to write.

It brings me certain spirit. Like a brightness, every word to walk into your head deserves protection, a punctiliousness of manner that puts hiding everywhere—daylight in each corner of the room. For when was light a public thing? It surely lies instead as reclamation lies, in the empty space of each completed sentence, which lets grammar muse upon some possible nights it could have spent with grace. Darkness, after all, is too literal a hiding-space, pretending as it does to make a secret of the body: since secrecy annuls, eats up, what is significant in surface, it cannot be sufficient to our tastes. I remember how Ifat softened in the last summer that we met, the only time I ever saw her tire of melodrama's great good humor, the comic inspiration that allowed her to be both costumes and choreographer at the same time. Her body looked different, then, when she allowed her mind's fatigue to soften: the moment that her voice abstained from declaration and said instead whatever she felt must be said, privacy—like an uncanniness—clung about her voice, her face. She became more beautiful than her own beauty, a hard fight to have fought and won. I must recall the subtle trick she wrought upon her surface, so that giving in, henceforth, would be for me the folding of a garment that folds in order to declare itself a simple surface—shirt. That's what she made her personage become: the magic and mundanity of freshly laundered shirts. Or maybe I can make nothing else of her, not now, but some domestic joy. Brave heart, I say, like cleanliness you come to be undone, in the conviction you will begin again tomorrow. So no flowers for you this year, Ifat: already we have spent enough on fetishes.

And so I will not write as though I believed in the structure of a secret. Let infancy have secrets, just like fairy tales, but let at least the rest of us admit that we live deluged by the availability of significance—enough significance, in fact, to drown a spirit, to make it long to be cast up on some insignificant shore and lie there bleaching in sea salt, crying, "Cure me, cure me, salt"; "Mollusk, make me empty." To hide would be a gesture of spare courtesy toward the world, which surely knows that revelation must be a hiding, something quite as startling as a dream. I will not write as though the names of my parents were anonymities to me, suggesting lives I happenchance sit down to record: if they were not my parents, what would possess me to believe that they could be, to me, of such unfailing interest? Similarly, it makes little difference that, even as I write, Tillat germinates another child—it has been a slight inaccuracy on my part to claim that she has merely three, for a fourth will be among us before my sentences are done. It's no great matter: I shall write these tales as though she has just three, saving up my discourse to confer devotion on the child that's still to come. I will not mention Dale at any length, although great length occurs to me (be distracted, elsewhere, Dale, as you read through this shortest sentence). I'll not now find habitation, like enough, to give sufficient space to Jamie and describe the repose that settled between us as we went walking down a street. "Everyone looks like someone else," I murmured to him as we went walking down the street, amazed again to note that the world consists almost entirely of look-alikes, faces already known. Those days, the streets were flooded with Cory Aquino look-alikes, and each one that we met astounded us both, which suggested that walking with Jamie was one sure way of keeping my face exactly where it was, away from slippage into some third person. For faces slip, become third persons in their bearing of themselves, a disheartening trick to observe. I hate to see a fallen countenance, pieced back together in the pain of its visibility. It is like a night that petrifies at its significance as night, unable to disperse itself into rest's complicity. I will not choose to dwell on such a night: I plan to save my daylight.

The goodness of such a scheme begs, of course, an obvious question. "That's all very well," I hear some voice grumble, "but is daylight equally amenable to saving you? What if it tires of such assumptions of good cheer?" It does not matter, for daylight always tires, needing hours of afternoon where it can retreat—to read a book, perhaps—and pretend not to be day. Living in daylight, after all, is not so different from living between two languages: it is a lie to say that some people only live in one, for to know a couple of different languages is merely a matter of demonstrating the pangs of intimacy that beset our mouths each time we speak. Coming second to me, Urdu opens in my mind a passageway between the sea of possibility and what I cannot say in English: when those waters part, they seem to promise some solidity of surface, but then like speech they glide away to reconfirm the brigandry of utterance. So snatches of discourse overheard in the streets seem fraught with robbery, a low-income level making each voice belligerently protest, "I need, I need, a different speech!" Speaking two languages may seem a relative affluence, but more often it entails the problems of maintaining a second establishment even though your body can be in only one place at a time. When I return to Urdu, I feel shocked at my own neglect of a space so intimate to me: like relearning the proportions of a once-familiar room, it takes me by surprise to recollect that I need not feel grief, I can eat grief; that I need not bury my mother but instead can offer her into the earth, for I am in Urdu now. But just at the moment I could murmur, "the stillness of a home," Urdu like a reprimand disturbs my sense of habitation: "Do you think you ever lived on the inside of a space," it tells me with some scorn, "you, who lack the surety of knowledge to intuit the gender of a roof, a chair?" Surely I can live in courtyards, afternoons, I muse in departing, arenas of regressed significance—a soothing notion, genderless!

Living in language is tantamount to living with other people. Both are postures in equilibrium that attend upon gravity's capacity for floatation, which is a somber way of looking out for the moment when significance can empty into habit. For significance is that which must be bailed out all the time; it must be peeled away with onion tears in order that habit can come bobbing up like mushrooms on the surface of a soup. When I have lived with other people, one of me is always bailing out with a maniacal devotion, night and day; another of me with great forbearance weeps over the onions; while the last is on the crow's nest of my mind, clinging onto the expectation of the day when it can cry out, in some drama, "Habit ahoy!" It requires, of course, a certain hardiness of soul, to peel or bail at someone else's significance, given that another may not agree with such a structure of commitment. But then, the grace of habit. That, for me, is what the theater was, a commingling of habitation with habitual speech: to learn a part until it turned to habit was entrancing, particularly since I did not know any other space that could tell me quite so firmly, "You are just a part." The shape of a day was different, then, its length piecemeal, when group by group would rehearse a part until its measured sentences were done. My body felt synchronized with the posture of those sentences, one drawing from the other's discipline, disinterested to determine which was curtain and which empty space. We worked in a habit of desultory concentration through the day, so that nightly our performance became a dividend for the ways we worked apart in a self-repeating solitude. Night harvested our labors, bound us loosely in a sheath—suggesting that, rather than applause, we waited for the intensely perfunctory binding of our bodies into work. Elation came to me only once the night was over: rarely have I felt quite as at home as on a stage after the play is done. The lights are still on, but they are not performing; a set begins to break into ingenious shapes; the company now treads the floorboards with a curious ring of bodily peace, for they are walking on and off in quiet chitchat, each face fatigued, restful in its half-undress.

No, for me the theater had little to do with what glamour there is in performance: performing was only part of our work as we set about to collaborate in the production of a habit, learning the sweet peace of saying someone else's lines. Now I feel that a classroom requires far more exertion of performance, putting you in charge of an ostensible script but withholding the serenity of plots that end—that may fall apart, or perhaps trail off, but do finally end—uncomplicated by the threat of future resumption. Theaters resume nothing, and even though it made me curious to see how Friday's play would feel inevitably new on Saturday, my profession in that era was, I knew, based on discrete time: if the bane of teaching is a "to be continued" sentence, our solace was that theater resumes only to repeat. I was not called Suleri in those days, for my father the orator felt wary of allowing his name to be associated with such public frivolity. It would interfere, he felt, with its single-minded linkage to the genesis of Pakistan. I did not mind being called this other thing, although as I watched my Pakistani audiences from town to town, I could tell they were less interested in genesis than in the stage: it made my heart pang for Papa. He could not, however, know about those audiences, for some principle of fidelity prevented him from being part of them; he never came to see me work. But on some nights when I came home fatigued—wearing the necessary serenity of a body engaged in work, in habit—he would look at my face and say, almost wistfully, "Tonight, you acted well?"

I could not separate the well from the good in that time, my body from sensations of well-being. For if theater taught me to repeat, to be habitual, I had still to learn the subtle practice of distraction, when a mind prevails on will in the manner of wind dispersing light so that an elemental privacy is most discernible where the elements cohabit. My mother, enchanting in abstraction, never lit a cigarette until the sun was set. When I was small enough to need her presence by my bed before I slept, her habit lit upon me as I would wait for the revelation of the shadow of her lips—a vision rhythmic, unexplained—in the habit of her smoking. If I lay in waiting long enough before sleep fell on me, then I could catch the tenor of her mouth in the tiny illumination of her cigarette: it was startling to me, piercing, to grope at what I saw, making me repeat, "She is not where she is; she has gone somewhere different." It took me years to conceive of distraction as a mode of possible attentiveness, a subdivision of habit that could function in the world of people as an attitude most kind. But I liked my mother's ability to evict concentration out into the air that she inhabited, so that her watching was also a veiling, a gesture of respect. She was slight and had an open forehead that functioned as a screen upon which we could read the comings, leavings of her sympathy. Her eyes were brown, but age and absentmindedness put lightness in them: they turned green, to me they looked quite green, on the occasion of our last encounter. "You know," Ifat gravely told me, "when Shahid came home, he needed to hold her, pull her into his arms . . ."—I listened—"but I could not touch, I could not even look." For my mother had entered her final habit of distraction. "I miss her," Ifat sighed.

Such thoughts make spirit abstracted, like a cigarette, although I do not wish to make my mother analogous to nicotine. No, I will not write as though my habits had a source, particularly when my reference is to a woman so disinterested in origins. The theater had more to do with smoking: it knew full well the joy of taking something into the body that can within a second be removed, smoke behaving then like someone else's lines. Last year, when I decided to sit down and write a series of short tales, I imagined those tales would wend their way into a final story, to be titled "The Last Cigarette." Renouncing vice seemed like a suitable accoutrement of finality, a gesture of purity perhaps, making me anticipate the triumph with which I could write, "I have smoked my final cigarette." Apparently, I hadn't. At the nether end of habit, the dark side of its moon, addiction rarely countenances such a clean completion: it refused to be complicit with my desire to believe I can see some things to their end. Ending, vice told me with courtesy, has little to do with starting again, which reminded me of how I first learned to write Urdu. When we were children, we learned to write that magnificent Persian script with pen and ink, upon a wooden board. Our boards—*takhts*—were lap-sized slabs of wood, their surfaces smooth with dried clay. Each morning, after we had written on our boards, we had to dampen lumps of clay and rub them smoothly on the letters we had written and then leave our *takhts* drying in the sun. They lay out in the courtyard maturing for the characters that in the morning we'd inscribe, at noon, wash away. I so loved that ritual that sometimes when I write today, I long to pass a lump of clay—wet and smelling heady—over my own inscriptions, rhythmically covering over "The Last Cigarette." Smoke like clay smells pleasing in its freshness, and both are gray, but when has neutrality of color signified what one can or cannot obliterate?

I used to think that our sense of place would be the first to go, after the hurly-burly of our childhood's constant movement. We would not pay much attention to our setting, I believed, but would dwell on face instead. For a while it felt quite true, so that during my sojourn in the American Midwest the vast strangeness of the place to me was humanized by such a presence as Dale's face, just as in my first horror at the unmitigated prettiness of Williamstown I could turn to the grayness of Anita's eyes for some amelioration. But now I must admit that my faces do not remain distinguishable from their contexts, that their habitation must lend feature to the structure of significance. It is hard for me to picture Nuz without seeing simultaneously Karachi's maniacal sprawl, its sandy palms and crazy traffic. Shahid looks like London now, in the curious pull with which London can remind, "I, also, was your home." Tillat in desert-land is busy, surrounding herself with oases, pools of infancy, converting in my mind a grain of sand into signs of impressive fertility. And it is still difficult to think of Ifat without remembering her peculiar congruence with Lahore, a place that gave her pleasure. "It's blossom-time and nargis-time," she wrote to me in her last letter, "and what a lovely city it is—a veritable garden." Then, after a quick catalog of domesticities, she added, "I love you, Sara, the times I've felt, 'if Sara were here, how much easier it would be . . . '" We had reached by then an age of feeling comfortable with our compliments, glad to be saying everything as often as we could; so I would not have paid her comment particular heed, were it not for the deranging circumstance that attended on my reading. When policemen came to take that sentence from me, I darkly knew that my task of reclamation would keep me working for some time to come, and that by the time I had got them back, those words would be my home. And not just my residence: I made a city of that sentence, laying it out like an architect as a picture of the parameters where I could rest, or shop, or work. In simpleheaded fealty, I worked at making Ifat my geography, my terrain of significance, on which I thought, and slept, and breathed. Now context becomes a more abstracting thought, admitting finally: you never lived in Ifat anyway; you live in New Haven.

The place, I must confess, has a certain brand of charm: in terms of its advantages, no one can blame us for being too bucolic. New Haven cultivates instead an open gloom that seems happy to acknowledge disrepair and the superfluity of appearance. It does not pretend to be a place where people eat or spend their leisure in wide spaces, uncloistered; it believes rather in the virtue of a dark interior. There are plenty of those about the town—dark buildings, twice-locked gates—and we are entirely accustomed to getting up in the morning and stumbling over homeless bodies huddled on our floors of ivory. At first its penury appalled me, until I realized that what cramped the town was the weight of unwritten volumes: they scored lines of unfinished writing on every second face that walked the streets, creating almost audible nocturnal sounds of a hundred machines at work, grinding to produce massive printouts of anxiety. It made me feel compassionate. "There, there," I wished to say, "let be." But gradually an air of comradeship grew up between us, until my life learned to make allowances for the city's grimness; it, for me. At work I practiced feeling consternation about using up my xerox quota for the year, about being wanton in my use of envelopes and letterheads. And I enjoyed meeting my colleagues as we went on companionable prowls through Linsly-Chittenden Hall—a building notoriously unsafe—going from classroom to classroom in search of bits of chalk. "I can understand stealing tables or lecterns," I marveled, "but chalk?"

New Haven thus allowed me to congratulate myself on my own bravery, as though I were living in a war zone again: certainly the police cars do very well at replicating the shriek of air-raid sirens. On fanciful days I can imagine that I am back, listening to the brigadier bark out his commands, in the pink house on the hill. Or sometimes, in a room that looks aslant on the gothic roofs of Yale, the architecture of the academy—that proliferation of cupola and dome—deranges into something different in my eyes, offering me a landscape that sometime in its history was devoted to making mosques with irregular metallic domes, representing an Islam I do not know. Then the city dissonance seems in collusion with some shrill Quranic cry, as though destiny has again placed me, as it always will, in a Muslim country. In those moments I am glad to go out wandering again, breathing in the intellection of the West, feeling in the air a heavy peace of books unwritten and books written, never to be read.

So many books will now remain unread. The one I most regret is *Boys Will Be Boys*, my father's life and times, since I doubt that he will ever write it now. For a while he planned to write it in Urdu, and I undertook to translate it into English: what labor of elation that would have been for me! I am sorry that I will not read a book about the stern and secretive life of breast-feeding, another one that will not be. But I can't say it makes me sorrowful that Fawzi never finished her passionate romance, that those days are gone when she kept polling all her friends for adjectives pertaining toward nipples: "corrugated" was the best she found. "Only Fawzi," sighed our friend Dale, "would begin a passionate romance with a description of a dying dog." The book was set in Africa and called *A Corner of the Sun*: my favorite moment in those fifty pages was when an old African doorman gazed at Fawzi's heroine to say, "She no number-two type lady. She number-one type lady": perhaps I do regret that sentences of such

183

caliber will never see the light of day. My mother, who seemed to speak in written sentences, in a modulated and yet easy prose, would never write. I know she should have written—today I would feel more protected if I knew that somewhere about the house I could pick up my mother's book. On the score of writing, however, I think she had unconsciously imbibed the sentimental honor of the East, which sees a book in all that it admires. When the poet Iqbal was offered some honorific title by the literati of India, he refused to accept it until they had first bestowed a similar glory on his former teacher. "But what has he written?" asked the literati, scandalized. "I," replied Iqbal, "am his book." Mamma appreciated such a tale, so if some higher authority ever questions her, I can easily imagine her replying, "I wrote Ifat and Shahid; I wrote Sara and Tillat; and then I wrote Irfan." "I have written nothing," groans my father, "done nothing with my life," while we are sitting in a house in which at least two rooms are given over to stacks of newsprint and his impetuous prose. Such quirks of belief make me feel compassionate in New Haven, when often I wish to impress upon my friends a different sense of the tangibility of work. Writing disappears, I say, in reference to my father's trick of life; sometimes it happens in the strangest settings, when you think you are asleep; take solace from the fact that—try as you will—it cannot go away.

For writing is the tricky milk that runs like metaphor through *Shab-e-Miraj*, the Night of the Heavenly Ladder. It is the night when Muhammad did a speedy Dante, climbed up with Gabriel from hell to heavens in such short space of time that his wife Ayesha is reputed to have claimed, "His body was not missed." Two things are crucial about this night: when offered water, milk, or wine, Muhammad chose a cup of milk, to indicate his fondness for the middle path; then he did some rapid negotiations about the numerical value of prayer. God wanted him to make his people pray fifty times a day, but as Muhammad turned to leave, "Are you mad?" Moses hissed to him, "it can't be fifty—they have too much to do!" So Muhammad interceded on behalf of the pragmatics of life, and God conceded some, again and yet again, until they cut it down to five. "Still too many," said Moses disbelievingly. But Muhammad replied that he could not go back again, for he would feel ashamed. I remember a cross-legged tailor sewing curtains in our house first telling me that story: he nodded with approval at his prophet's shame. Sometime later, Ifat heard the old folktale which declares that if one prays throughout the night on *Shab-e-Miraj*, one's water turns to milk. "Which water," I said slowly, when she came to me brimming full of schemes, her eyes singing, "We are going to do *something* tonight, tra la la la la." But even after I heard that she meant drinking water, I still felt dubious: "But Ifat," I asked, "how can I pray all night when I don't know how to pray?" "Then let me be your Gabriel!" came her pleased reply. "Don't you remember, Muhammad up on that hill when Gabriel came and said, 'Read,' and Muhammad said, 'I cannot read,' and Gabriel said 'Read,' and Muhammad said he couldn't, and this went on and on until Gabriel said, 'Read in the name of your God, who has created man'—a horrid phrase—'from clot'?" Yes, I remembered that old story. "Then I'll be your Gabriel!" she exclaimed, as though there were no further question. "I'll teach how to pray!" When I tried to remind her that *she* did not know how to pray—let alone teach—it already was too late, for Ifat's shoulders were determined, arched with wings.

Did we pray? I remember suppressing sniggers over books like *The Right Path* or a translation of the Quran by someone called Marmaduke Pickthall as we lay awake long after our designated hour of sleep. Periodically, Ifat would send me running to turn on the bathroom tap: "Ifat, it's still water," I called out. When I returned to notice how dejected she had become, like an angel hunching over with the weight of wings, I tried to rally round, saying, "Never mind, I always hated milk." "So do I, but that's just not the point," said Ifat gloomily. "You can't look a gift cow in the udder, not when it's a miracle." And so we turned back to our books, looking for tales that pleased us both, sitting together companionably on Ifat's bed—perhaps the ladder did descend at some point in the night, but only after God had sent us dozing off, to put us in the wrong. In the absence of Ifat's miraculous companionship, today I would not dare wait up for or care to will a startling change upon my night: I am content with writing's way of claiming disappointment as its habit of arrival, a gesture far more modulated than the pitch of rapture. In any case—although I did not know it then—to fall asleep on Ifat's bed was milk enough, to sleep in crumbling rest beside her body. Sometimes like water she runs through the sentences of sleep, a medium something other than itself, refracting, innocent of all the algae it can bear and capable of much transmogrification. Her water laps around me almost in reproach: "You were distracted, when I requested your attention. You were not looking. I was milk."

In October, when I turn back the clock, I know we must sleep deftly before we recollect that tomorrow, night will come before its hour. It cannot matter. Bodies break, but sometimes damage feels a necessary repair, like bones teaching fingers how to work, to knit. When my bone broke, I was perplexed: was I now to watch my own dismantling body choose to unravel with the cascading motion of a dye in water, which unfurls to declare, "Only in my obliteration will you see the shapes of what I really can be?" I felt put out of joint by such a bodily statement, then chastened to imagine the arduousness of what it must mean to scaffold me: poor winter tree, put upon by such a chattering plumage, castigated out of season for its lack of green! Put upon by sentences galore—like starlings, vulgar congregations! In pale and liquid morning I hold the Adam in me, the one who had attempted to break loose. It is a rib that floats in longing for some other cage, in the wishbone-cracking urge of its desire. I join its buoyancy and hide my head as though it were an infant's cranium still unknit, complicit in an Adam's way of claiming, in me, disembodiment.